NO BUGS!

NO BUGS!

Delivering Error-Free Code in C and C++

David Thielen

Addison-Wesley Publishing Company
Reading, Massachusetts Menlo Park, California New York
Don Mills, Ontario Wokingham, England Amsterdam Bonn
Sydney Singapore Tokyo Madrid San Juan
Paris Seoul Milan Mexico City Taipei

Many of the designations used by manufacturers and sellers to distinguish their products are claimed as trademarks. Where those designations appear in this book and Addison-Wesley was aware of a trademark claim, the designations have been printed in initial capital letters.

The authors and publishers have taken care in preparation of this book, but make no expressed or implied warranty of any kind and assume no responsibility for errors or omissions. No liability is assumed for incidental or consequential damages in connection with or arising out of the use of the information or programs contained herein.

Library of Congress Cataloging-in-Publication Data

Thielen, David.
    No bugs! : delivering error-free code in C and C++ / David Thielen.
      p. cm.
    Includes index.
    ISBN 0-201-60890-1
    1. C (Computer program language) 2. C++ (Computer program language)   I. Title.
    QA76.73.C15T53 1992
    005.26'2--dc20
                                   92-14802
                                      CIP

Managing Editor: Amorette Pedersen
Set in 10.5-point Palatino by Benchmark Productions

1 2 3 4 5 6 7 8 9 -MU- 9695949392
First Printing, September, 1992

To my parents,
Mickey and Cynthia Thielen—
You gave me more than I can ever repay.
I love you.

Table of Contents

Preface   xv

Chapter 1 Introduction   1
   Attempt 1   1
   Attempt 2   2
   Who This Book Is For   3
   No Bugs   4
   Testing   5
   Why This Book   5
   More Tricks   6

Chapter 2 What is a Bug   7
   Where Bugs Come From   8
   Tricks of the Trade   9
   Finding Those MFUs   9
   Create a Priority List   10

Chapter 3 General Principals   11
   Debug Code is Read-Only   11
     Debug Code   12
     Debug Macros   12

Using Debug Macros   12
Proper Use of DEBUG   13
Exercising Code Paths   14
Trap Macros   14
Use of IntTest and Trap   15
Walking Each Path   16
Forcing Actions   16
Rock-Solid Low-Level Functions   18
Debugging in Conditional Defines   20
Using the value of DEBUG   20
Using the Variable   21
Comment Your Open Issues   21
BUGBUG   22
Keep It Unobtrusive   23

Chapter 4 Some Basic Tricks   **25**
TestAll Functions   25
TestAll Function   26
Using TestAll   27
Restoring System State   27
When Your Program Exits   28
ENTER/EXIT Logging   29
ENTER and EXIT Macros   29
Using ENTER and EXIT   30
Inline ENTER and EXIT   31
Error Message File   31
Object-Oriented Programming   32
Filling Buffers   32
Freeing a Structure   33
Filling Buffers   34
NULL Pointers   35
Prototyping Including CONST   35
Prototyping Examples   36
CRC Checking   37
Roll Your Own   37

Chapter 5 Assert the World   **39**

    Assert to the Rescue   40

        Assert Macro   40

        Assert a String   41

    AssertBool   42

        Assert a Boolean   43

    AssertInt   43

        Assert an Integer   43

    AssertStr   44

    Assert a Structure   45

        Structure IDs   46

        Assert a Structure   47

    Parameter Validation   49

        memcpy.c   50

    Assert Everything   52

Chapter 6 Debug Printfs   **53**

    Message Box   54

    Debug Printf   57

    Conditional Printfs   59

        Conditional Defines   59

        Using Variables   60

        bugcheck.h   61

        Debug Check   61

        Debug Printf   61

Chapter 7 Watching the Stack   **63**

    Stack Space   64

        stckfill.c   65

        stckused.c   65

        chkstk.asm   66

Chapter 8 Watching the Heap   **69**

    The Concepts Behind the Code   69

    Some Details   70

Allocate Some Memory   71
    Alloc.h   72
    AllocChkHeap and AllocHeapWalk   73
    Alloc   75
    AllocFree   77
    AllocRealloc   79
How to Use the Memory   81
Be Sure All Freed   81
    AllocDone   81
Asserting a Pointer to the Heap   82
    AssertHeapPtr   82
EMS and XMS   83
Handle Tracking   83
    HdlCreate   84
    HdlAdd   85
    HdlFind   86
    HdlExist   86
    HdlDelete   87
    HdlNext   88
Expanded Memory (EMS)   88
    EmsCheckHdl   90
    AssertEmsPtr   91
Extended Memory (XMS)   92

Chapter 9 File I/O   **93**
Consistency Checks   93
Assertion   94
Open   94
Check Handle-Based Calls   97
    Handle Check   97
    Errno Check   97
Seek   98
Read   99
Write   101
Close   102
    FilesDone   104

Chapter 10 Special Tricks of C++   105

Override Global New and Delete   105
  New and Delete   106
Constructors and Destructors   107
  String Constructor   108
  String Destructor   109
Base Class Assert   110
  Base Assert   110
  Base Dump   111
  String Assert and Dump   111
A Debug Class   112

Chapter 11 Special Tricks for Assembly Language   113

Trap and IntTest   113
  TRAP   114
  jc Example   115
BUGBUG   115
  BUGBUG Example   115
Checking Registers   115
  Check Registers   116
  TrashReg   119
  ConstReg   119
Creating Local Variables   120
  Local Variables   121
Wrapping It All Together   122
  Complete Function   122

Chapter 12 The Testing Process   125

Developers and Testers   125
Warts and All   126
Setting Up the Process   126
The Plan   127
  Automation   128
  Bug Reporting   129
  The Bug Database   130
  The Testing Process   133
  Internal Testing   133

White-Box Testing   133
Black-Box Testing   134
Designing the Tests   135
Running the Tests   136
Testing Platforms   137
Testing, Testing   138
The Beta Test   139
When to Beta   140
When to Ship   142
Selecting Beta Sites   142
Handling Bug Reports   143

Chapter 13 Shipping the Product   **145**
To Release or Not To Release   146
Management   147
Putting It All Together   148
Dire Warning!   149

Chapter 14 Useful Bug-Discovery Tools   **151**
Bounds Checker   151
Microsoft Test   153
MemCheck   155
Multiscope Post-Mortem Debugger   157
Windows Dr. Watson   158
Windows Debug Version   159
RT-Link   160
Debuggers   161
Periscope   162
Soft-Ice   163
Multiscope   165
New Tools   166
Remember   166

Appendix A Debug Message Boxes   **167**

  debgmsg.c   167
  _errnum.h   171
  pop_box.c   172
  tty_box.c   176

Appendix B Debug Second Monitor   **181**

  debgprnt.c   181
  mda.c   191

Preface

As a rule, no one works in a vacuum. Writing this book was no exception. First and foremost, I would like to thank my wife, Shirley, both for her support in helping me write this book, and in general, for marrying me. I would also like to thank my two daughters, Winter and Tanya, for allowing me to work occasionally when I should have been playing with them.

This book is filled with tricks I have picked up over the years. Some I have figured out by myself; others are stolen from other developers. I owe particular thanks to Gordon Letwin and Mike McLaughlin, from whom I learned quite a few of these tricks, and to Andy Barnhart, Scott Quinn, and Pete Stewart.

I would also like to thank a number of other programmers with whom I have worked over the years—not just for ideas on writing bug-free code, but for making me a better developer through their ideas, their feedback, and their friendship. If I tried to list all their names I would forget someone, so I'd like to extend my general gratitude to the people I work with at Microsoft and those I used to work with at Harris & Paulson. Special thanks to those at DTS, my first company.

Special thanks also to Microsoft Corporation, a wonderful environment for a software developer, and the place where I learned about a testing system that really works (MS-DOS 5.0). As I reach each mountaintop, I find ever greater heights to scale.

A secret, until now known only to very few people, is that my writing is terrible. Fortunately, I have been able to work with individuals who have turned my raw text into something not only readable but, I hope, enjoyable to read. The only reason you will be able to understand what is in this book is because Jean Zimmer turned a group of awkward sentences into flowing and understandable prose.

I showed the first draft of this manuscript to a number of people; their comments helped me to change the book for the better. This group of people includes Aaron Ogus, Joe Hayes, Marianne Jaeger, and Paul DiLascia.

I also want to thank the people at Benchmark Productions and Addison-Wesley, without whom this book would not have been published. This group includes Chris Williams, Amy Pedersen, and Andrea Mulligan.

Finally, "Domo arigato gozimasu" to the editors at Village Center (Japan), whose encouraging response to my "No Bugs" article in their magazine, *C Journal*, led me to write this book. Without their feedback on the article I would never have written this book. This thanks includes Tak Nakamura and Sano Koji.

Special thanks to Eric Hough, without whom the companion disk would never have been done.

The ultimate test for any book is its ability to help you, the reader. I hope you find this book lets you write code that has fewer bugs. And more important, I hope this book makes writing bug-free code easier so you can spend more time on the fun parts of developing . . . the next killer program.

Dave Thielen
Redmond, WA
March 1992

Chapter 1

Introduction

Attempt 1

We've all been there. We've finished up our new application. It's been copied and shipped out the door. It's arriving at the steps of our first customers—and the phone rings.

The call starts as a technical support question. But the problem escalates, and pretty soon it becomes obvious—there is a bug in the program.

And not just some little insignificant bug that users can work around—this is a big hairy bug that gets right in the face of each and every user and stops them from using the program.

It doesn't matter how many customers you have; having to replace 100 percent of the copies of your program is a horrendous expense. And the cost is not just limited to replacing the disks. You now have a reputation for delivering buggy software. This reputation will cost you sales for the next several years—perhaps enough that a product that would have succeeded will fail.

If you cringe every time the phone rings after you ship a new product, then this book is for you.

Bugs can have more than just a financial impact. The most common program in the world may be in use in a cardiac care unit in a hospital. A small failure in a copy program could change a number in a loan application. A vertical market application may have a business person reporting incorrect information to the government (which happens to be a felony). Somebody's word processor was used to type up the specifications to the airplane you are flying in.

People may come to depend on your programs in ways you never foresaw or intended. But they *do* depend on these programs. And just as you expect the airplane you are flying in to not come apart in midair, people expect their programs to operate correctly, no matter what the circumstances.

Users now expect software that is virtually bug-free. Over the next several years, they will demand this robustness in all of their programs.

Attempt 2

I recently had a bug in some code reading from a data port. Even though I was reading the data one byte at a time, every once in a while my buffer pointer would be off by two. It was driving me crazy!

I placed assertion checks throughout my code to make consistency checks. And the same thing kept happening—the code would pass the tests until suddenly it was off by two. I finally asked a coworker to take a look at the code. After studying it for a while, he came back and said he saw nothing wrong, assuming the function calling me hadn't set the direction flag (we're into x86 assembler here). To make a long story short, the function calling me did not guarantee to clear the direction flag. It's just that it was usually clear.

This bug could have easily slipped through—I wasn't even testing properly for it. In an environment such as ours, we make assumptions (such as n = 1 + 2 will give us 3). Unfortunately, our assumptions are things that are *almost* always true.

To add insult to injury, a summer hire porting this same code came in and pointed out that I didn't clear the direction flag. I showed him where I had done it earlier in the code and then told him about spending a day determining that I had to do it. He told me I just should have shown it to him first, which is unequivocal proof that summer hires should be tortured.

In another case many years ago, I wrote a program that included a weird kind of word processor. Because of the requirements, the file format of the word processor was quite complex, and we had some bugs in the code.

This was in the early days of the PC, and I didn't have all the ideas presented here to use in writing the program. There were some bugs in how we were handling the file format. I knew that much, but I still couldn't seem to find the bugs, at least not all of them. In desperation, I put code in to check the consistency of the file and to correct the file when it found problems. As time went on, I found additional bugs in my regular code, which I fixed and added to the consistency checks and error correction.

While I kept reducing the number of bug occurrences, I couldn't eliminate them. Finally, to make testing easier, I ripped out the consistency checks and error correction—and the bugs went away. I had apparently fixed the original bugs, but bugs in my "bug fix" code had introduced totally new bugs.

And then there are the horror stories I've heard about other companies. . . . (Thank God there is always someone doing something dumber or worse than you.)

There was one company where they preferred not to test the product because they would find bugs and then they would have to fix them. Of course, when the users reported the bugs, they had to fix them anyway.

At another company, management would write schedules, dictating when all bugs were to be fixed and, on that day, by definition, there were no remaining bugs. (Of course, there were lots of immediate "enhancements" that users requested, which were implemented shortly after shipping.)

Who This Book Is For

Most developers know that software is inherently buggy. And most developers also want to eliminate these bugs before shipping a product. *No Bugs!* is written for these developers.

However, writing code without major bugs (sorry, we haven't yet reached the point of truly bug-free code) is a team effort. It takes the work of more than just the developers. It takes testers, managers, support personnel, and other people. This book is for these people too.

No Bugs! is designed to solve a problem: buggy code. Because it is aimed at the problem instead of a specific audience (for example, just developers or just testers), parts of this book may not be interesting to certain audiences. Chapters 3 through 10 are written mainly for developers. Chapters 11 and 12 are written mainly for testers.

Keep in mind that this book is meant to be read straight through. If you want to develop bug-free code, you have to understand all of the processes that go into getting there. Developers need to understand the test process. Testers need to understand what the developers do.

Most important, the managers and other people responsible for ensuring that the whole process works need to understand all the details of the process. They need to serve as the gatekeepers and see that the process is actually being followed.

Finally, this book is written from the Windows/DOS/PC perspective. While most of the ideas discussed are generic to any computing platform, many of the implementations are specific to the PC. And some of the code is specific not only to the PC but to specific compilers (stack checking has a tendency to be that way).

However, even if you program on a platform other than the PC, in a language other than C, you will still find this book valuable.

No Bugs

Almost all software developers agree on two things: software development takes too long and software is too buggy. With the advent of graphical user interface (GUI) applications, this situation can only get worse. Not only are most programs adding functionality (more to test), but the message-based architecture has changed it from difficult to impossible to test all command combinations.

While this book is titled *No Bugs!*, it does not tell you how to write bug-free code. Everyone uses the term *bug-free* like some kind of mantra, but it just isn't possible to have entirely bug-free code with today's tools and technology.

This book focuses on teaching you how to deliver code with as few bugs in it as possible. Just as important, it also focuses on giving you the knowledge to discover what bugs still exist in the program before you ship it.

The process of eliminating bugs breaks down into three steps:

1. Putting the bug in the code (yes, *you* put it there)
2. Finding the bug
3. Fixing the bug

In *No Bugs!*, I attempt to minimize the first step, putting a bug in the program. By reducing the number of bugs you put in code as you write it, you can dramatically shorten the amount of time necessary to complete and test the program. Most of the tricks presented in this book do not actually stop you from writing buggy code. You will still make the same mistakes you made before, but your program will wave a red flag upon discovering a bug. This immediate notification that you have made an error will allow you to fix it quickly and painlessly.

Most of the tricks described here are quick and unobtrusive. Everyone knows writing bug-free code is critical, but many developers are loath to spend time eliminating bugs when they are working on a tight time schedule (with managers breathing down their necks). These tricks are designed so that the hurried developer will want to use them. With a few hours of practice, you can implement most of the enclosed code samples, and you won't really see any of this new code until it finds a bug.

Testing

An important and often ignored part of the code-writing process is testing. Every nontrivial software program, no matter how simple, contains bugs. Every testing process, no matter how thorough, lets some slip through. However, the final determiner of a program's relative "bug freeness" is the testing process it is put through.

Chapter 12 discusses testing. The PC industry has matured greatly over the past several years. What would have been considered rock-solid several years ago is now considered so bug-ridden as to be worthless—and a worthless product is not purchased.

A good testing strategy can help you deliver a product that is rock-solid under seemingly impossible circumstances. The MS-DOS version 5.0 operating system offers an impressive example of what a thorough, intensive testing strategy makes possible: MS-DOS 5 was designed to run on every existing PC system, regardless of the system's hardware and software. It had to run on PCs built before anyone was sure what compatibility meant, and it had to run with TSR (Terminate and Stay Resident) combinations that were presently running only via luck. Thanks to an extensive testing process, MS-DOS 5 was shipped without a single significant bug. Microsoft shipped a solid product.

By setting up and following a good testing system, you can ship a solid product. If you ship a product and have to cross your fingers, you can be pretty sure its bugs will come back to bite you.

Why This Book

This book is designed to teach methods for writing code that is as bug-free as possible. Complete, fully functioning code examples would have expanded this book to an unacceptable length, so I have included illustrative code fragments only. Several examples of full code follow in Appendices A and B.

This book also gives you all the information you need to create your own debugging code, but it doesn't provide the actual code. You may order a disk that includes complete source code. Ordering information appears at the back of the book.

More Tricks

This book in no way lists all the tricks currently being used. It merely lists those that I have invented or learned of. If you have some ideas of your own, please let me know about them.

Chapter 2

What is a Bug?

This is the most important chapter in the entire book. The seemingly simple question, "What is a bug," actually has a very complicated answer. This chapter is devoted to answering that question.

A developer I know once said, "Bugs should not be called bugs, they should be called Massive Fuck-Ups (MFUs)." The word *bug* implies that some outside agency decided to infest your program with bugs, and that if you live a clean life and sacrifice small, furry animals at the foot of your computer, they will go away.

The truth is that MFUs exist because programs are written by people, and people make mistakes. The only way to eliminate MFUs is to go into your code, find the bugs, and fix them.

This is the most critical concept to understand and the one most often blown off. You *will* write MFUs. You *will* sit down, and even with the best of intentions, you will put MFUs in your code. Think about it—you *know* that you are the one putting the bugs in there. And somebody needs to find them so you can remove them. No amount of designing, prototyping, CASE, reviewing, management, and so on will avoid this.

This concept is important because it colors your approach to debugging your code. If you view mistakes as bugs, you hope none are found. (You hope the good fairy came by, sprinkled some pixie dust around, and the bugs didn't like it and left.) If you view the mistakes as MFUs, you know without doubt that they exist, and you try to find all of them so that they can be fixed.

It is critical that developers and managers feel good, not bad, when MFUs are discovered. They should worry if they don't find any. Instead of assuming your program works and waiting around for someone to prove otherwise, you should take for granted that it doesn't work and search diligently for the bug that will make it fail.

So, for the moment, you have to accept that you will create MFUs in your code. (I sure manage to put a lot in *my* code.) I don't know of any way to avoid doing so. The trick is to find the MFUs and correct them as painlessly as possible.

As a side note, the term "bug" is so firmly established in the lexicon of developers that I see no way for "MFU" to replace it. However, I think it is important that you occasionally refer to bugs as MFUs. This will remind people that bugs are placed in the code due to a developer's mistake.

When developers insist that bugs are not MFUs, you should worry. Why? Because that means the developers have abdicated responsibility for ferreting them out and fixing them. This is when it's critical to remind them that bugs are MFUs. It's much harder for developers to avoid responsibility when they are told there is an MFU in their code than when they are told there is a bug in their code.

So what is a bug? Well, if you run a program and it formats your disk (assuming you are not writing a format program), most people will agree that a bug did it. From this point on, opinions start to differ. I hear statements like: "No one uses that feature, so it's okay that it will trash the hard disk" "Just tell them to buy a parallel port printer" "They can override the result, so its okay that it doesn't add up correctly"..., "That's not a bug, that's a feature!" The people who say these things and find them acceptable in the programs they write are the same ones who will turn around and say that the bad design in a program they bought is a bug.

By my definition, if a reasonable person expects certain functionality and it isn't there, or expects a program to work in a certain manner and it doesn't—there is a bug.

Where Bugs Come From

How do bugs get into a program? Very simply, you put them there. You are the one who sits down and types some buggy code into your program. It does *not* sneak in on its own. You might mistype a line. You might use a wrong variable. You might copy some code from elsewhere that doesn't quite work. In any case, it is *YOU, YOU, YOU.*

Every time you code, you insert bugs. This is one of the dirty little secrets of programming. Programmers write code and create bugs every day. Good coders are generally really good at creating bugs. (This is so our employers have to keep us around to fix all of the bugs later. COBOL programmers learned this years ago.)

Tricks of the Trade

This book does *not* contain any tips on how to stop creating bugs. It *does* contain tips on how to make bugs more obvious. A bug that always crashes the program is preferable to one that crashes only one system . . . the one located in Siberia. If a bug always crashes the system, you fix it immediately. If it only crashes in Siberia, you might get sent there to fix it (possibly without a return ticket).

Every C programmer has undoubtedly had to track down a loose pointer bug that wrote over memory that didn't belong to it. Later in the program, you may have found the bug when you used the memory that the loose pointer corrupted. You then had to work backward to see who wrote over the data. Wouldn't it be much easier to have a pop-up box notify you when the pointer first writes over the data, informing you immediately that you have a bad pointer?

A bug that causes a message box to pop up, stating that a problem exists, is preferable to a system crash. The trick is to catch a bug as soon as something goes wrong, not discover later the problems it has caused. The message box can't fix the bug for you, but at least it can tell you that something is wrong.

The next chapters describe a number of practices that I have developed over the years to help me debug my code. The important thing about these practices is that you implement them while you write the code. They help you weed out bugs as part of the actual development process rather than after the product is turned over to testers, or even worse, users.

These practices reveal bugs that might otherwise be hard to find, making development faster and easier. They also find bugs that you might otherwise spend hours, or even days, trying to fix. By minimizing the number of bugs that are initially written into code, these practices make it easier to find the remaining bugs. In most cases, these "tricks of the trade" eliminate certain classes of bugs.

Finding Those MFUs

Given the level of complexity in today's programs, especially those written for message-passing architectures such as that of Windows or the Macintosh operating system, it is impossible to test for all the many combinations of uses. Instead, you need to test each message in such a way that you feel confident it will work in combination with any other set of messages.

By using the tricks described in this book, I have drastically reduced the bugs that make it to the testing stage. I have also spent a lot less time debugging and a lot more time coding. I not only get more done, I also spend less time kicking myself because I can't find a bug. More important, the code I generate is solid. A bug or two still might get through to testing, but the bugs that do get through generally appear only if a very rare, specific sequence of events occurs.

If you use these tricks, you will be able to generate more code with far fewer bugs. It is critical, however, that you implement these tricks as you go, not after you are done. You might be surprised at how easy early debugging becomes. When you have a mistake, a pop-up window tells you what you did wrong. And you will rarely have to track down some subtle bug that takes days to discover.

Create a Priority List

The best way to start fixing bugs is by prioritizing jobs. Which is more important, adding a feature or fixing a bug? For example, suppose you're aware of two faults with your word processing program: it lacks a print feature, and it has a bug that keeps it from finding words beginning with "z." You prioritize by deciding that adding a Print feature is more important than fixing the Find feature.

Create a priority list. Call it "bug list," call it "to-do list," call it anything you want, but maintain only one list for all jobs. (If you have two lists, you have to decide which task to take care of if there is time for only one of many.) By keeping one list, you will know, in order of importance, which bugs to fix and what features to add prior to shipping. Without this knowledge, you can only hope that everything will come together, luck will ensure that the right features are added, and the bugs will be magically chased out of the program.

Chapter 3

General Principles

Starting with this chapter, we'll discuss how to develop code in such a way as to minimize bugs. The principles discussed here hold not just for the methods described in this book but for almost any other tricks you may invent yourself. For nonprogrammers, this chapter is definitely optional. For developers, this chapter is a "must," because it lays out the general principles to follow when implementing all of the tricks listed in the following chapters.

Debug Code is Read-Only

A common problem I have seen is the program that runs fine with debugging turned on but blows up with debugging turned off. (Debugging can be turned on and off in many ways, as we will see later in the book. However, the most common method is the use of **#ifdef DEBUG** and **#endif**.) I even know of one commercial program that was shipped with debugging turned on, but its **debug printf** disabled because it wouldn't run in non-debug mode.

This problem generally occurs because the code, in its debug checking, will return from a function if it determines that an incorrect parameter is passed. However, if debug is turned off, the same checking does not occur, and the function does not return an error.

There is a simple solution to this. All debug code should be read-only. This means code reads data but never writes to it. Just as important, however, is that debug code does not affect the code path. The debug code is executed, but it never causes the subsequent code path to change. Debug code is the equivalent of calling a function that returns void.

All debugging code should be placed within an **#ifdef DEBUG** so that the testing can be turned on and off. In addition, put all functions used exclusively in debug mode within **#ifdef DEBUG** so the function doesn't exist in the final version of the program. The linker will then let you know if you are still calling debug code with debug turned off.

Debug Code

```
#ifdef DEBUG
void DebugCheck (char *p)
{
    ...
}
#endif
```

Using macros leaves your code a lot cleaner. You can define the debug macros inside a **#ifdef DEBUG**, and then define a macro that generates no code for the **#else**. Instead of **#ifdef DEBUG** statements littered throughout your code, you have just the macros, and the result is cleaner-looking code. The example below illustrates the use of these macros.

Debug Macros

```
#ifdef DEBUG
#define          DebugMacro(p)          DebugCheck (p)
#else
#define          DebugMacro(p)
#endif
```

Using Debug Macros

```
// clean:
    p = GetBuf (0);
    DebugMacro (p);
    WriteBuf (p);
```

```
// too busy:
  p = GetBuf (0);
#ifdef DEBUG
  DebugCheck (p);
#endif
  WriteBuf (p);
```

It is critical that the debug code treat the application's data as read-only. Implement the use of the debug code so that it makes no difference what code is executed outside the **DEBUG ifdefs**. If the debug code fixes data or causes a different path to be taken through a function, when the debug code is removed (or undefined), you will have a different program—and your debugging will have hurt instead of helped you.

If your debug code finds a parameter error, the debug code should not cause a return from the function. If you want to run the same error checking in nondebug mode, the correct method would be to run the same check again in your nondebug code after the debug check, and then return. The point of the debug code is not maximum speed or minimum size but maximum debugging.

The program below illustrates a code path that is read-only and one that isn't. Notice that in the incorrect example, the function can handle a **NULL** pointer passed in only if **DEBUG** is turned on.

Proper Use of DEBUG

```
// correct (read-only):
#ifdef DEBUG
  if (! pSrc)
    DebugPrintf ("Source String NULL\n");
#endif
  if (! pSrc)
    return (NULL);          // We handle NULL even if DEBUG is off

// incorrect (not read-only):
#ifdef DEBUG
  if (! pSrc)
    {
    DebugPrintf ("Source String NULL\n");
    return (NULL);     // you will now die when DEBUG is off
    }
#endif
```

Exercising Code Paths

The hard-to-find bugs generally occur only under rare circumstances. (After all, if a program reboots your system every time you run it, you will usually fix that error.) Some of these rare cases are caused by executing a code path that has never been executed before. When your program first starts, you will generally do a **malloc** or two. There is a code path you can take if the **malloc** fails (you don't assume it succeeds, do you?), but has it ever failed?

If not, you have an accident waiting to happen. What does your program actually do when that particular **malloc** fails? If you haven't exercised a code path, you haven't fully tested your program. *Be sure that you exercise every code path.* If you have an "**if** () ... **else** ..." and you have always executed the **else** part, then the **if** part is a bug waiting to happen.

The easiest way to make sure all code paths have been exercised is via two macros, **Trap** () and **IntTest**. **Trap** () will advise the tester if the expression in the parentheses is true, and **IntTest** will advise the tester regardless of the result. For each conditional (**if, for, while, do, and switch**), put a combination of **Traps** and **IntTests** so that you will hit a **Trap** or **IntTest** for each possibility.

When you hit an **IntTest** or **Trap**, you can do one of two things: you can do a **printf** when you hit that particular code path. Or you can place an **int 3** so your debugger will stop at that line of code. If your debugger is a source-level debugger, there is no need for a **printf**. When the debugger pops up, it will tell you where you are.

If the **if** contains increments (**i++**), function calls, or other code that cannot be executed twice, put an **IntTest** in the **else**. If there is no **else,** put one in for debugging. The program example below illustrates the use of these macros.

Trap Macros

```
#ifdef DEBUG
#define        IntTest        _asm { int 3 }
#define        Trap(t)        ( (T) ? _asm { int 3 } : )
#define        TrapNot(t)     ( (T) ? : _asm { int 3 } )
#define        IntTestElse    else _asm { int 3 }
#else
#define        IntTest
#define        Trap(t)
#define        TrapNot(t)
```

```
#define            IntTestElse
#endif
```

Use of IntTest and Trap

The program example below illustrates the use of the preceding macros:

```
TrapNot (i > 0);
if (i > 0)
   {
   IntTest;
   i--;
   }

Trap (i <= 0);
TrapNot (j > 0);
while ((i > 0) && (j > 0))
   {
   IntTest;
   i--;
   }
IntTest;

if (i++ < 100)
   {
   IntTest;
   j--;
   }
IntTestElse;
```

If the **if** is not executed, **TrapNot** will notify you by dropping you into your debugger. If the **if** is executed, **IntTest** will notify you. I use an **int 3** to put me in Soft-Ice (the debugger I use) for each of these. Then I walk through the function to ensure that the code path works correctly. Once you have tested a code path, remove all the **Traps** and **IntTests** that you hit while testing the path.

As time goes on, you will find fewer and fewer **Traps** and **IntTests** remaining. You will then have to devise special tests to actually force those paths to be hit.

Once you have exercised all possible code paths, you may not have ensured that all possible combinations of code paths will work, but you will know that each subpath has at least been tested.

Walking Each Path

Walk yourself through each code path in each function. You do not have to walk through every combination of paths, but you should walk through every part of each function. Watching the affected variables as you single-step through functions often makes a bug stand out.

Sometimes you can move quickly as you walk through, and other times you might want to watch several variables at each step. Use your judgment. Much of the time, simply watching the program run and focusing on one or two variables allows you to single-step through quickly. Then suddenly the code will do the opposite of what you expect on a conditional, and you must pay very close attention to everything.

Unfortunately, there is no set of rules that tells you how careful to be and what to watch for. The one rule I almost always follow is that the first time I go through a function, I look at all the parameters on entry, single-step through very carefully, and check the parameters on exit. On subsequent passes through a function, I generally check only those items that are affected differently by the new code path that caused me to hit a **Trap**.

As your code nears completion, you will find some **IntTests** and **Traps** still in your code. Just because no one has ever exercised that code path before is no reason to simply pull them. You should develop special test cases to exercise those paths. This is a critical step.

Forcing Actions

Another set of bugs that occurs rarely is due to system functions that usually act one way, but sometimes will act another way. The most common case is a **realloc** call that, under ordinary circumstances, will return the address passed in. However, occasionally, it returns a different address.

If, during your testing, the **realloc** always returns the same address, you have no way of testing to see if your code properly handles a different address being returned. You not only have to worry about the variable you pass to **realloc**, but also about whether another variable is also holding a pointer to the old (pre-**realloc**) address.

However, if a **realloc** always returns a different pointer in debug mode, you know your code will handle that properly. In addition, the **realloc** needs to put garbage data in the old memory location. Otherwise, a pointer to the old location will continue to see legitimate data until that memory is used again.

Whenever you unlock relocatable memory, move it and, if possible, put garbage data at the old location. If you are caching disk data, as soon as it is unlocked, write it to disk and clear the buffer. If you are interacting with a TSR on the timer tick and there are times you set a semaphore to turn the TSR off, call the timer interrupt on the instruction before and after turning the semaphore on, and on the instruction before and after turning it off.

You also want to create an impossibly bad environment for the program. If it survives, it should survive any actual situation in which resources become a little tight. RT-Link, a linker that provides code swapping, does this beautifully. You can run it with one available code page so all code is swapped into the same page. This ensures that every code page will get swapped in on top of the previous code page. If any code page depends on another code page being in memory at the same time, it will crash the program.

On any call, if an error can occur, it should be tested. Every **malloc** should be tested for returning a **NULL**. Not doing this is criminal, because you will cause intermittently noticeable errors only on low-memory systems.

Every file open should test for a handle of -1, including creating temporary files. You should also test all file I/Os for success. I have seen programs that assume that a temporary file create-and-write always succeeds. I guess the developer's RAM drive was always big enough, but mine wasn't. You even need to check read/writes to existing parts of a file. If a net connection drops, you cannot access the file.

For one DOS program I wrote, I created a virtual memory system that would go first to regular memory. If regular memory was used up, it would go to EMS. If EMS was used up, it would go to disk. So how did I know it all works? I set it up in debug mode to (optionally) always allocate from EMS or disk. The disk-only version was slow (we're talking big delays on a 486), but all the functions worked. In this manner, I was able to force the program to use each memory system.

If your temporary files are moved to a hard disk when a RAM disk fills up, be sure to test your application with a RAM disk that is too small. Anywhere you have created backup procedures to protect you in case your preferred resource fills up, be sure to test the entire system using the backup resource.

If you write a TSR that uses semaphores to prevent reentrance, then just before and after the semaphore, call the interrupt on which the TSR is sitting to be sure it will not reenter itself.

The trick is to see if you can break your own code. All of these tricks are specific to the code they are testing. Every program will have different weak points. You need to find those weak points and break them. If you are determined to discover those MFUs you put in your code, then you will be able to figure out how to break your code.

Rock-Solid Low-Level Functions

When you add two integers (assuming the result isn't bigger than an integer), you know that it will work. Think of how debugging would be if you didn't know this. You would have to check what the **add** instruction did at each place you added two numbers, and test each instance with various combinations of numbers. Basically, you couldn't program.

Now, let's move up a level. What if you aren't positive about **strcpy** (or any of the run-time functions)? You now can at least program—in fact, I remember the early days of PC compilers when you couldn't depend on these functions—but it isn't an easy task. Your testing and debugging job has grown by leaps and bounds.

But you can trust the processor and run-times. (If you can't, it's time to switch.) Every program has a set of low-level functions that are specific to it. These low-level functions have two important attributes. First, they are used throughout your program. A minor bug in one of them is a serious MFU in the program. Second, you can generally test all possible combinations of program flow in them.

Thoroughly test these low-level functions. You should be able to depend on these calls the same way you depend on a + (add). The best way to do this is to write test programs that will call your low-level functions with enough different parameter combinations to test all possible code path combinations, and print to the screen only if the return value is incorrect. That way, when you make a change to the function, it's very easy to test again.

You have two major gains from exhaustive testing of the low-level functions. First, part of your code approaches test bug-free. Having part of your code bug-free should drop the total bug count. More important, although a bug in a high-level function will generally cause one problem, one single bug in a low-level function (such as linked list management) can cause innumerable other bugs to appear throughout your program. The low-level functions are the foundation and framework of your program: if they're solid, the program is solid. If they're shaky, no amount of effort elsewhere can make the program solid.

It is also critical that this testing be performed on *all* functions that are widely used, even if they are not lowlevel. If these functions don't work, you'll get bad data at times, and the rest of your program will fail. Although you may not be able to come up with a complete test suite for something like an edit window, you should still test it thoroughly. If it has a bug, you will see it everywhere in your program.

When is a function low-level enough to merit this exhaustive testing? When it is possible to come up with a set of test cases that will exercise every possible combination of entry data. Any function that can be tested this way should be. This is the single most important step you can take to have bug-free code.

The remaining code might have logic errors (that is, it does not do what you intended) rather than bad code (resulting in, for example, a loose pointer). Logic errors are usually easier to find, and if they slip through to shipment, they are usually easier to work around.

(By the way, one of the two major advantages of object-oriented languages, their bug-free classes—is a result of extensive testing of low-level functions. The functions might not have test routines, but they have probably been used by enough people in enough ways so that all of the bugs have been wrung out.)

If you take another look at your code, you may be surprised by how much of it you can test this way. You can test practically every command in a database, every function in a word processor, every tool in a graphics package. When you view the program logic, it becomes clear that a small number of test cases will exercise all the possible combinations of paths through the code.

If you find you can't test anything this way, that all of your functions depend on all the other functions, then you've got a serious problem on your hands. However, if you've written really clean, separable (that is, object-oriented style) code, you will find almost all of your functions can be exercised in this manner.

So you have a giant library of code, and you don't want to write test routines for all of it. So don't. You can write test routines for sets of 15 to 40 similar functions (for example, **strcat, strcpy, strlen**) in about three days. You will find few, if any, bugs. However, those you do find will be bugs you were never able to reproduce before. And if you find no bugs (assuming you wrote good test programs), you now *know* that your low-level functions are solid.

If most of your code can be tested this way, you may be pleasantly surprised by how few bugs make it into the final product.

It may be coincidence, but when I started all-out testing of my low-level functions, that's when I saw the biggest decrement in bugs in the programs I wrote. Not only that, but after I began doing this, I can't recall a single instance where a bug that seriously affected the entire program was found.

Debugging in Conditional Defines

To maintain speed, you will probably not want all of your conditional error checking to be compiled. Some of the error checking can take an extremely long time. (Generally, a specific check does not take a lot of time; rather, the check is called often.) Also, if you are printing debug information to a terminal or second monitor, you don't want useful information to be scrolled off the screen by other information in which you have no interest. Sometimes, the sheer volume of printing can slow down the program because a monitor can write to the screen only at a certain pace, and no faster.

You can take either of two primary approaches to this problem. The first is to not compile in the extra debug code. This is much faster because the debug code just doesn't exist, but you will have to recompile if you decide you need some of the debugging prints back. The program example below illustrates the use of conditional compiling.

Using the value of DEBUG

```
#ifdef (DEBUG >= 2)
   real_slow_test ();
#else
#if (DEBUG >= 1)
   slow_test ();
#else
#if DEBUG
   fast_test ();
#endif
#endif
#endif
```

The second approach is to test a flag at the beginning of the debug code and skip it if the test fails. If the flag is a variable, you can change its value in your debugger. Doing so makes it easy to turn the debug **testing/printfs** back on part way through the program, or turn them off after you no longer need them.

Using the Variable

The program example below illustrates the use of a debug variable:

```
#ifdef DEBUG
  if (DebugVar >= 2)
    real_slow_test ();
  else
    if (DebugVar >= 1)
      slow_test ();
    else
      fast_test ();
#endif
```

Although there are a lot of fancy ways to implement this conditional debug code, two rules seem to hold. First, you usually don't ever want to turn debugging on or off after a compile. Second, both ways of implementing this seem to be equally fast to code and execute.

For simple code, debugging is generally an on/off proposition. In these cases, using **#ifdef DEBUG** alone is probably sufficient, and anything more is a waste of time. For code that is otherwise simple but has a couple of time-consuming checks, you can use the value for which **DEBUG** is defined as conditional compiles.

With conditional debugging, keep in mind that some debug tests are matched. If your **malloc** conditionally sets the signature bytes before and after each region of allocated memory, it must do it if any of the conditional defines that check the heap for the signature bytes are executed. I once spent several hours trying to determine why some buffers were failing their CRC tests; the reason was the CRC creation code had been **ifdef**'ed out while the checking hadn't.

Comment Your Open Issues

As you code, issues or questions come up in certain pieces of the code. Will a function work on a Super VGA monitor? How do you handle data files with a particular error? Do you need to watch out for a certain error condition?

These questions are not resolved by **Traps** and **IntTests**. Rather, they are items that you have not fully coded for, or, in some cases, you have not coded for at all. In other cases, your program will fail under conditions in which you expect it to continue running.

There are possible logic errors that occurred to you at one time or another. Unfortunately, the human mind being what it is, these errors will be quickly forgotten . . . until the bug report comes in. These MFUs are classified as *"Oh shit!"* bugs. This highly technical language is based on the phrase usually uttered when the bug is first reported to the developer responsible.

The place to write down these concerns is in the code itself. Anywhere else, and these cocerns can get lost. If it's in the code, it's there forever, or until you resolve the question.

In these cases, place a one-line comment, the word **bugbug**, followed by your initials and the date. You can follow this with a comment that runs for several lines, but the first line should give a reasonable description. The program example below illustrates the use of the BUGBUG comment.

BUGBUG

```
// BUGBUG DNT 3/21/92 - No memory. Should we go to disk?
// At the moment if we run out of memory we fail. However, if this
// runs on large files, running out of memory could be common.
```

This **BUGBUG** accomplishes three things:

- By performing a **grep**, or text search, for **BUGBUG** on all the files, you get all the title lines of open issues. (Note: in the **asm** chapter, a way is shown to have the **BUGBUG**s print to the screen during a compile. Unfortunately, C doesn't support printing during a compile in a manner that makes this possible.)
- The open issues travel with the code. You can't lose the list of open items— unless you lose the code too.
- The open items are right there at the relevant spot in the code—you don't need to search all the files to find the correct spot.

When you ship a product, you should not have any **BUGBUG**s in your code. In the example above, you may have decided to go to disk. You may also have decided you could limit yourself to memory. In either case, the question was resolved.

If you don't use **BUGBUG**, you may forget or lose important issues. You may not remember the issue until users report the bug after the program ships. Using **BUGBUG** is simple, and it's more time efficient than recording the information elsewhere.

Keep It Unobtrusive

Keep your debugging as unobtrusive as possible. The rest of your program should be affected hardly at all by debug code. (The program might run a tad slower, and the user might see a pop-up debug message.) Good debug checking stays hidden, out of the way, until it finds an MFU.

Chapter 4

Some Basic Tricks

Now we get into the actual programming tricks. This chapter includes all the tricks that don't need a chapter of their own. This isn't to say these tricks aren't important, merely that they can be explained in fewer words. Chapters 4 through 11 list specific tricks and how to implement them. The tricks are described generically. The code is C (and Assembler where required) for the PC. These tricks do not add to your work—they *do* save the time you previously spent debugging.

TestAll Functions

Suppose your program is mysteriously crashing. You don't know why or exactly where. What you do is place the **TestAll** function at various points in your program. You are now able to narrow down the bug. **TestAll** reports all is okay and then, 20 lines later, reports an error. The bug is in those 20 lines.

So what is this magical **TestAll** function? Quite simply, it calls every global test function you have. At a minimum, it checks the **NULL** memory locations, the entire heap, and the amount of stack left. It also asserts all global data structures. In Windows programs, it calls the **ValidateCodeSegments** and **ValidateFreeSpaces** functions.

TestAll Function

The program example below illustrates the implementation of **TestAll**.

```
void TestAll (void)
{

  // Test system
  TestHeap ();
  TestStack ();
  TestNull ();
#ifdef WIN
  ValidateCodeSegments ();
  ValidateFreeSpaces ();
#else
  TestEms ();
  TestXms ();
#endif

  // Test global variables
  AssertBool (bInsertMode);
  AssertDbase (&MainDbase);
}
```

Whenever you create a test function that can be called anywhere (globally) to perform its test, that test should be added to **TestAll**. Eventually, **TestAll** becomes very slow, and because of that you rarely want to call it. However, it proves invaluable in two places:

- When your program completes a major task. (For example, a word processor saves one file and is about to open another.) It is invaluable because you are switching data sets, and you should know which data set doesn't work.

- When tracking down a bug that could be due to anything. It is a quick way to identify the bug. You place the **TestAll** function at various places, beginning at a point where you know the system is still okay, and going up to the point where you know it is trashed. **TestAll** will not only find where you first start to mess up your program, it will also tell you which test failed, which helps you identify what is wrong, and where.

In the example below, **funcBad** blows up due to an error in the system, but the code looks error-free. By using **TestAll**, you can determine which function is causing the problem. Before walking through **funcBad**, you can see if **func1** or **func2** is actually the culprit, although you don't see the bug's effects until **funcBad**.

Using TestAll

The program example below illustrates the use of **TestAll**.

```
funcMfu ()
{

    funcOk ();              //You know this function is okay
    TestAll ();
    func1 ();               // Might have a bug
    TestAll ();
    func2 ();               // Might have a bug
    TestAll ();
    funcBad ();             // See the bug's effects
}
```

Restoring System State

We have all seen situations where the program itself runs well, but DOS always seems to lock up shortly after use. For instance, there was a program I used to use regularly with no apparent bad effects whatsoever. However, when I ran it in a Windows DOS box, every time it started it would cause a Unrecoverable Application Error. Obviously, it was playing with memory that didn't belong to it.

When your program is about to exit, you should fully test the system. Many programmers don't worry about an error message on exit, thinking that, after all, this is only exiting—who cares if things are a little bit wrong?

This is a very dangerous practice. First of all, many of these errors are symptoms of bugs that, under different configurations or use, could cause problems while you run the program. Second, many of these errors are damaging to the operating system. If your program returns to DOS but DOS locks up five seconds later, it's still your fault.

Be careful to test a program's exit under all conditions. In DOS, if you don't watch for CTRL-C, be sure you are called when the default CTRL-C handler exits the program. Under Windows, you need to check when closing your application and when Windows itself shuts down while your application is active.

When Your Program Exits

At the time your program exits, follow the procedures listed below.

1. Call **TestAll**. This single call should test the integrity of your system.

2. Call the **StackUsed** function (discussed later). This call will tell you the maximum amount of stack space used. Every time you exit the program, print out both the maximum stack size used and the total stack size. This gives you constant feedback, letting you know whether you have set your stack size appropriately.

3. Compare the interrupt table and any other operating-system global variables, such as parts of the BIOS data area that are of interest, to ensure that you have left the system as you found it. This is not a concern under Windows unless you are writing some *very* dirty code—in which case, this is the least of your problems. Bounds Checker (discussed in the Tools chapter) will check both the interrupt table and the BIOS data area on exit to see if you have changed any of it, so there is no sample code here for this. However, if you don't use Bounds Checker, you need to write a program that saves the interrupt table on start-up (before the C-run-time initialization code runs). Then, on exit, compare the existing table (after the C-run-time **_end** function runs) with the saved table.

4. Leave the system in the state in which you found it. This is critical to ensure that your program does not swallow up resources every time you run it. Any files that have been opened should be closed. Any DOS, EMS, or XMS memory you have allocated should be freed. This is critical for EMS and XMS memory because DOS itself will not free that memory on exit. Also, if this memory is not freed, your program is probably wasting resources while it is running.

5. Check your heap for allocated memory that is not freed. If you use both the near and far heaps, be sure to check both. Memory that is not freed when you finish an action generally indicates a logic error. Even if the only problem is that you forgot to free a pointer, you are still eating up a scarce resource.

6. Check for files that are still open. This might also be indicative of a logic error. However, open file handles, in addition to being a scarce resource like the heap, are much more dangerous if left open: first, if

the system crashes, part of the file is still in memory instead of on disk, and the file can be corrupted. Second, if another application wants to access the file that you have opened with an exclusive access, you have locked out the other application.

7. If you are running Windows, make sure you have freed up all resources. Some Windows resources are still in very short supply. (For example, Windows has only five screen-device contexts.)

Most of the examples in this list are illustrated later in this book. However, some programs use resources that are not as general. Be sure you have freed up all those resources.

ENTER/EXIT Logging

A sometimes useful practice is to log the functions you call. This logging is written to a debug terminal and/or to a debug file. Essentially, it gives you a running list of what function you are in, and where you were called from.

It can also be used by a debugger to track your call stack. This allows the debugger to list, by function name, the calls you made, beginning with main, to get to your present location.

The most common method is to make the first line of every function an **ENTER** macro, and an **EXIT** macro the return. The **ENTER** macro prints that the program is entering the function. The **EXIT** macro prints that the program is leaving the function and returns from the function.

You will see the use of **__FILE__** and **__LINE__** below. These are constants defined by the compiler. **__FILE__** is the file being compiled, and **__LINE__** is the line of the file being compiled. Using these constants, you can give the source location of a **debug printf**.

ENTER and EXIT Macros

The program example below illustrates the definition of **ENTER** and **EXIT** macros.

```
#ifdef DEBUG
#define    ENTER(func)      DebugPrintf ("Entering %s (%s:%d)\n",\
                            func, __FILE__, __LINE__);
#define    EXIT(func)       DebugPrintf ("Exiting %s (%s:%d)\n",\
```

```
                                    func, __FILE__, __LINE__);
#else
#define      ENTER(func)
#define      EXIT(func)
#endif
```

Using ENTER and EXIT

The program example below illustrates the use of **ENTER** and **EXIT** macros.

```
char *strcpy (char *pDest,char *pSrc)
{

   ENTER ("strcpy");

   while (*pDest++ = *pSrc++)
      ;

   EXIT ("strcpy");
}
```

However, this method leaves a lot to be desired. First, where were you called from? If a function does not implement **ENTER/EXIT**, the function it does call will appear to have been called by a higher-level function. Second, a given function might call **strcpy** from many places, some of which might be in loops. The question is where was a specific **strcpy** called from? Finally, if a function exits in multiple places then, you have to place the **EXIT** macro in all of those places.

A better alternative is to create a macro for calling a function. The macro will print that the function is being called, and include the file and line number of where it is being called from, by using **__FILE__** and **__LINE__**. The macro will then call the function. Finally, it will print that the function returned, optionally including the return value.

The below example will work for any C++ program. However, most of the C compiler vendors are also putting the capabilities required for this (scoping) in their C compilers.

Inline ENTER and EXIT

The program example on the following page illustrates the use of **ENTER** and **EXIT**.

```
#ifdef DEBUG
#define     StrCpy(d,s)          (ENTER ("strcpy (%p, %p)", d, s,);\
char *r; r = strcpy (d, s); EXIT ("strcpy = %p", r), r)
#else
#define     StrCpy(d,s)          strcpy (d, s)
#define
```

In this example, **ENTER** and **EXIT** are functions. Functions can track how deep the function is nested, and indent the **printfs** appropriately. They let you see the matching **EXIT** for an **ENTER**.

Regardless of how you set this up, be sure you don't drown in data. Also, if the logging occurs on every function call, including those to the low-level library calls, your program can slow to a crawl. (It will spend a lot of its time spewing vast amounts of data to the debug terminal, virtually all of which is ignored.)

So when should you use this? Personally, I have never found **ENTER/EXIT** logging useful. I list it because it is a technique some people use. However, my recommendation is that, unless you see a real return in doing it, you should skip **ENTER/EXIT** logging.

Error Message File

You will probably want to send most of your debug output to a second monitor. In some cases, however, you might want to send it to a log file. The easiest way to do this is to have the **DebugPrintf** decide whether **printfs** are going to the monitor, the file, or both.

The error file needs to be opened when the program first starts. You may want to either create the file (deleting the previous log file) or use a new name each time (such as incrementing the extension until you find a filename not in existence) so that you are not creating too large a file.

You then need to consider committing (DOS function **ah=68h**) the file on each write. If you don't do this and the program locks up, you lose the most recent writes—usually the ones that tell you why the program locked up. However, a commit on each write is slow. And you can't use your RAM disk—it's lost if the system locks up. I have found that writing to a log file, with enough information and commits to be useful, is so slow as to be useless.

If you do choose to use an error log, under DOS 4.0 and above, you can open a file using the extended open so that all writes are committed. Use an error log; it's lots faster than calling commit file (DOS 3.3 and later). Do this only under DOS 4.0 or later, if at all.

Object-Oriented Programming

Object-oriented programming (OOP) is the buzzword of the moment. It will solve all of your programming problems, give you unlimited wealth, and make you irresistible to the opposite sex (actually, unlimited wealth will do that too).

While the subject of OOP merits a book of its own, here we will discuss how OOP can help stop bugs from ever showing up, and just what parts of OOP give you these advantages.

OOP does not require any specific language. You can write OOP code with assembly language. But using a language like C++ forces you into a number of object-oriented practices, and makes some other practices very easy to implement.

At the simplest level, OOP means keeping your functions separate. For example, functions that handle circles have no code or data in them for squares. Code for squares has no code or data for circles. Code for drawing an item has no code or data for circles or squares, but it knows how to call the circle or square drawing functions.

Separability in your program makes it easy to implement exhaustive tests for virtually all the functions in your objects. Separability also means that a change in one object doesn't affect any other object. Use an OOP approach to your coding. It will pay off in a much-easier-to-test product.

That said, realize that OOP is not a panacea. It makes it easier to do some kinds of testing, but it does *not* eliminate the need for any tests. It also adds some new bugs that you normally don't see in C or ASM.

Filling Buffers

Another bug that rarely makes its presence felt occurs when you use buffers before they have been initialized or after they are freed. When you do so, the buffer will usually retain the correct data. But at other times, the buffer will have legitimate data, although not the data it should. This leads to very subtle bugs.

Whenever a buffer is considered empty, fill it with an ID byte (or string, if you prefer). This ID byte should be a value that is invalid for the structure being filled (-2 usually works for everything). By doing this, if you access the buffer after filling it, you will probably get data that is so very wrong that it causes an immediately visible MFU.

This is a very valuable trick to use before file reads. It ensures that you handle the end of the file when you get a successful partial read. Filling passed-in buffers is also a good check to make sure the passed-in buffers are long enough. If a function returns a string, and one of the parameters is the maximum length of the string, filling the buffer first will guarantee against bugs if the passed-in buffer is too short.

Also, when you free up a buffer, fill it prior to freeing it. This prevents bugs that are created by accessing a freed buffer that holds old data. Do this not just for freeing a buffer you have allocated, but also for internal cache buffers, data structures, and so on.

Anytime you are through with any kind of memory, fill it before freeing it. By filling freed memory, when you access this memory, you guarantee that you'll get bad values, thereby causing an obvious MFU. If you don't fill the freed memory, when you access it, you will see those bugs only in those rare cases where the memory is reused before you can fill it.

Try several values for **DEBUG_FILL_CHAR** at different times. In some circumstances, zero is deadly; in others, it's totally benign. Test your entire program using **0x00, 0x7E,** and **0xFE**. I have found **0xFE** to be very damaging in most cases. I don't use **0xFF** because -1 usually has a special, sometimes benign meaning.

Freeing a Structure

The program example below illustrates the use of filling a buffer.

```
// Include file contents:
#ifdef DEBUG
#define       DEBUG_FILL_CHAR      0xFE
#define       DebugMemSet(p,n)      memset (p, DEBUG_FILL_CHAR, n)
#else
#define       DebugMemSet(p,n)
#endif

// .c file contents
LinkListDelete (elem *p)
{

    // Take p out of the linked list
    (p->next)->prev = p->prev;
```

```
(p->prev)->next = p->next;

// Fill p
DebugMemSet (p, sizeof (elem));

// Add p to free list
p->next = pFree->next;
pFree->next = p;
}
```

The example above cannot only be used for memory but also for disk I/O. If you delete a record in a database file, filling the deleted record will guarantee that you get bad data if another record is still pointing to the deleted record. In short, fill anything that persists after the free/delete function returns.

Before any read, not just from disk but from anywhere (RS-232 port, and so on), fill the buffer with the ID value. Then if the read returns with no error without actually reading anything, the buffer will not contain any previous content that might have carried over from a previous successful read.

If the read is partially successful (that is, you read the end of a file), the fill performs a second function. If you assume all reads are fully successful, you will get bad data. Otherwise, you are probably using the same buffer to perform all reads, and the remainder of the buffer may hold what appears to be legitimate data.

You don't need to do this prior to a **MemCpy** or other direct memory copying. However, whenever you think someone else may fill a buffer for you (DDE, networks, and so on), you should fill the buffer first.

Filling Buffers

The program example below illustrates filling a buffer prior to a read.

```
MyRead (int iFile, void *pvBuf, unsigned uNum)
{

   DebugMemSet (pvBuf, uNum);
   return (read (iFile, pvBuf, uNum);
}
```

I have found it helpful to set registers that I use in assembly language modules to this same ID value. In higher-level languages, you generally don't have scratch global variables. (You can, but it's a terrible practice.) The idea is to fill any variable of any type before someone else sets it, or after you are done with it.

NULL Pointers

What discussion of eliminating bugs would be complete without discussing the use of **NULL** pointers?

On the 8086 (regardless of memory model) in C you have two **NULL** pointers, **SS:0** and **0:0**. In some cases, where DS is different from SS but DS is fixed, you also have **DS:0**. For other processors, you might still have more than one **NULL** location.

Regardless of the quantity of them, on start-up, copy the four bytes from each **NULL** to a global variable. Then, when the program ends, compare these values to the values at each **NULL** location. Write a message to the tester if they don't match.

Even though most compilers perform this checking for you, you should also do it yourself. There are two reasons for this. First, most of the compilers test only for overwriting **SS:0**. Second, you should have a **TestNull** function to add to the **TestAll** function. This allows you to test for **NULL** overwrites at times other than program exit—critical to narrowing down when you wrote to **NULL**.

Keep the following thoughts in mind: First, sometimes the **NULL** value will legitimately change. If you set an address on **int 0**, the **NULL 0:0** changes. Also, some compilers set **DS:0** to zero and then use that pointer for literal strings that are empty. Therefore, writing to **DS:0** can cause some unpredictable behavior.

Prototyping Including CONST

There is a certain type of bug I used to see a lot. I would spend hours tracking it down, and then I would finally find it. I would have done something like pass an **int** when I was supposed to pass a pointer to an **int**.

I did this so often that as soon as the compilers started doing prototype checking (I'm showing my age here), I always prototyped my functions. For a very small effort, you get a very large return on your investment.

C is designed to help you do anything you want. Most important to this discussion, it has the ability to use function prototypes and perform very strong type checking. Use prototyping. A good C programmer breaks the rules at times—carefully and deliberately.

All functions should be fully prototyped. This includes using **const** whenever possible on the prototype for function variables. Also, **void *** should be used whenever appropriate (such as in **malloc**, **memcpy**, and **read**) when it is legitimate to pass in or return any type of data. However, do not use **void *** when a function normally accepts only one type (such as **strcpy**).

Prototyping Examples

The program example below illustrates the use of proper prototyping.

```
void*malloc (size_t uLen);
void*memcpy (void *pDest, void const *pSrc);
char*strcpy (char *pDest, char const *pSrc);
```

All code should compile at the highest warning level with *no* warnings or errors produced. With C's casting capabilities, there is no need for any warnings.

This full prototyping has two advantages: First, if you see a warning, you know *something* is wrong, even if it's as simple as having forgotten to cast something. Second, it will catch a number of errors that otherwise might not surface for some time, errors that could take days to resolve. Prototyping rarely shows me where I have made a mistake, but when it does, it usually shows a type of bug that wouldn't normally show itself until much later when it would be very difficult to track down.

While most warnings can be resolved with a cast, that should be your last response. I once found a bug in someone's code where they passed a long (not a pointer to a long) when a function wanted a far pointer. Needless to say, this caused the function to bomb. When asked why the long had been cast to a pointer, the programmer replied, "To eliminate the warning message."

In most prototyping, if you use the void pointer where appropriate, there is virtually no need for casting. Unless it's clear to you why you do need to cast, you are, at the very least, doing something you don't fully understand. And writing code you don't understand is a guaranteed way to introduce MFUs.

The effective use of tools requires knowing when to use and when not to use something. For instance, a blow torch is a valuable and necessary tool for building cars, but it is not a recommended tool for repairing a circuit board. It's very important to know when the solution to a warning or error isn't casting, but is, instead, correcting your code.

CRC Checking

Personally, I have never seen the need for CRC checks. However, a developer I respect a lot swears by them, so I leave it up to you. I am sure there are times when they can pay off.

The first place to use CRC checking is on data structures, especially those that buffer generic data. By performing a CRC check, you gain two additional checks: First, if there is no way to make a consistency check (the buffer is from reading a binary file—any values are legitimate) of the buffer, you can still verify that the data is good. Second, if you want to make sure the structure hasn't changed to a different set of consistent data, the CRC will tell you if it's the data set we believe it to be, even if the data passes your consistency test.

Another useful check is to verify that you didn't write to the code or **CONST** segments. If you use Bounds Checker (see Chapter 14) or you are running under a protected-mode operating system (such as a Windows application in Standard or Enhanced Mode), it will do this for you. However, if you don't have these options, you can perform a CRC of these segments on start-up, and then compare it in your **TestAll** function and also when the program exits.

In both cases, this is usually due to a loose pointer. Keep in mind that some third-party libraries use a self-modifying code that makes this test difficult. However, with the chip pre-fetch queue in the 80286 and beyond, self-modifying code has become a dangerous practice that is being used less and less.

Roll Your Own

Keep in mind that this chapter is filled with suggestions, not a rigid set of practices to adopt as a whole. Some of these practices will work well for you, some not. You want to use those that pay off for you and not waste your time with those that won't.

In addition, if you have practices of your own that are not mentioned here, continue to use them. The key is to use what works, not what is written down. These tricks are ones to add to your repertoire, not replace it.

Chapter 5

Assert the World

A couple of years ago, I wrote some code that involved some very complicated actions on a buffer I was walking. I had several pointers, and if one of these pointers was off in relation to the others, I would get major errors.

I spent days on this code. Each time I found a bug, I tracked down its cause. Still, almost every time I fixed one bug, another was created. Finally, in desperation, I wrote a function that checked the pointers' relationship to each other at the beginning of each pass through the loop. If the pointers didn't match, I printed out the value of every local variable. The code I wrote was an assert.

Within a couple of hours, I found the remaining bugs and had the function working. I surrounded my assert code with a **#ifdef DEBUG** and left it in there. From then on, bugs in the code identified themselves.

Since then, I have come to use assert statements almost everywhere. Not only do they save you days of tracking down bugs, but they also find bugs you might otherwise miss. Further, for the asserts that never find a bug, you can feel that much more secure about your code—you have parts that you *know* are working correctly.

As you go through your code, there are places where you *know* that a variable holds a certain value, and there are places where you *believe* that a variable holds a certain value. And, unfortunately, there may be places where you *hope* that a variable holds a certain value (major MFU alert). Most of the time, the honest answer is that you believe a variable holds a certain value.

The fact that you don't know is part of programming. If you write a low-level function, you have no control over the code calling your function. In a complicated procedure, you believe that you understand every possible path the code can take, but you can't know for certain.

Assert to the Rescue

To solve this, make massive use of the assert capability. An assert function checks a Boolean expression, and if it is true, calls the warning message function. For example, you may place assert (**strlen(pStr) < 16**); just before you copy a string into a 16-byte static buffer. If a string is even longer than 15 bytes, the **assert** macro will print a message listing both the file and the line in the source code that caused the error.

Assert Macro

The program example below illustrates the use of a standard **assert** macro.

```
#ifdef DEBUG
#define    assert(b)    ( b ? printf ("##b in File: %s, Line: %d\n",\
                         __FILE__, __LINE__); : )
#else
#define    assert(b)
#endif
```

Most compilers support two asserts. One only exists if DEBUG is on, and the other exists even in the final released version. The first one is placed everywhere you believe the Boolean value to be FALSE. The second assert is placed only where you want the retail version of the program to exit if the Boolean value is TRUE.

This is bad coding—you've got MFUs in your program. There should be no assert in nondebug code. Under certain conditions, you might want to end your program. However, you should exit gracefully, putting up a message to the user that makes sense. How good will you feel about a program that suddenly exits to DOS with the line *internal error @ dave.c, line 253?*

This statement bears repeating because there are numerous commercial programs that ship with asserts in them. You need to handle all error conditions properly. Exiting to DOS with an incomprehensible message to the user is not acceptable. Give users enough information so that if it's 2:00 a.m. and they need to use your program to complete something by 8:00 that morning, they have some chance of figuring out what to do differently so the program will work. (End of lecture.)

You assume certain things either can't or must happen at certain places in your code. Place assertions in your code that test for these assumptions and will print if the impossible happens or the certain fails. The best way to place assertions is to look at your functions after you have finished coding them, and then ask yourself what can go wrong. Usually, one or more places in the code will jump out at you. Place asserts at these spots. While you're debugging, you're bound to come across bugs that can be flushed out by an assert. Place asserts at those points and remember the situation for the next time.

For example, if you assume multiplying two ints will always have a result that is an int, then **assert ((long) i1 * (long) i2) < 0x7FFF);**. As you walk through a tree, if you assume a certain pointer is always good, then **assert (pTree != NULL);** or **assert (pTree->uID == ID_TREE);**. One of the most important assertions you can use checks the ID in a struct when it is passed to, or returned from, a function.

Assertions are usually a low-investment, high-return effort. For any given data structure, you need to write an assertion function. Then you write a macro that will call the function if **DEBUG** is turned on, and will do nothing if **DEBUG** is turned off.

Anywhere you believe you have a pointer to the structure, or a variable holding the structure, but you aren't 100 percent sure, assert the variable. Generally, assertion code is fast, so load up your code with asserts everywhere. While you won't see much of a hit in speed, if an assertion fails, you are pointed right at the failure by module name and line number.

We break assertions into two parts: the code to check a data structure and the code common to all assertions. We will discuss the common code first.

C has had an assertion macro for years. If false, it will print out the false statement and the module and line number at which it occurred. We will get a little bit more sophisticated than that.

Assert a String

The program example below illustrates the use of a string assert.

```
#ifdef DEBUG
#define    AssertStr(pStr)    CheckStr ( __FILE__, __LINE__, pStr);
#else
#define    AssertStr(pStr)
#endif
```

Each structure has its own Check function. You can use an **assert** macro, but if you do, all the checking occurs in-line. This not only leads to a bigger program, but also makes complicated checking impossible.

If there is a problem in the Check function, the Check function calls a standard **AssertPrintf**. This is a normal **printf**, but it also passes in the __FILE__ and __LINE__ information. This way all assert **printfs** begin the same way. For example, in Windows, you use a Message Box and the caption can be **Assert - file: dave.c, line: 23**. The rest of the **printf** can be any formatted string that the Check function wants to display. The Check function should say what it didn't like, but don't worry about making it pretty.

Okay, we can print an assertion failure, but how do we know if we really do have a problem? The first part of the Check function is the code to check the data structure. This can be divided into two parts:

- Are you truly pointing at the data structure you think you are pointing at?
- Is the data structure holding valid values? Are the values consistent with each other?

Sometimes, you can't tell for sure whether you are pointing at the data structure. All you can do is see whether it holds valid data.

So you see how to check the big, complicated structures in your program. But what about simple data? Most code has a lot more ints and strings than structs. All you need to do is take a look at why you are using the variable. To demonstrate, in the following section, we will create an assert for a bool, int, and string.

AssertBool

You can assert a Boolean value very simply. The value of every Boolean should be either TRUE or FALSE. TRUE is defined as a nonzero value, but in virtually every program written, it has a specific value, usually 1 or -1. If Booleans are bytes, a Boolean with a random value has only a 1/128 chance of being TRUE or FALSE. If a Boolean is an integer, the odds against it randomly holding a legitimate value are even greater. So CheckBool can check for the values TRUE and FALSE. A Boolean with a random value will almost always fail this test. Although CheckBool isn't perfect, it does provide a lot of help.

Assert a Boolean

The program example below illustrates the use of asserting a Boolean.

```
BOOL CheckBool (char *pFile, int iLine, BOOL bVal)
{

  if ((bVal != TRUE) && (bVal != FALSE))
    {
    AssertPrintf (pFile, iLine, "BOOL = %d", bVal);
    return (TRUE);
    }
  return (FALSE);
}
```

AssertInt

An integer can hold any value. However, our stack routine (covered in Chapter 7) will be setting all ints to 0xFEFE. It's rare that an int will actually hold this value. You could set all uninitialized global ints to this value, too, and catch any cases where you use an int before initializing it. For the rare case where 0xFEFE is a possible value, just don't assert the int.

Most ints will hold a value within a range. If you are keeping a percentage count (like the install bars in most setup programs), the variable should be between 0 and 100. (It should also increase on each change, but that rule is specific to a count.) Therefore, you could add a minimum and maximum to the assert. If both are zero, don't check the range.

Assert an Integer

The program example below illustrates the use of asserting an int.

```
BOOL CheckInt (char *pFile, int iLine, int iVal, int iMin, int iMax)
{
  // See whether it has been initialized
  if (iVal == DEBUG_FILL_WORD)
    {
    AssertPrintf (pFile, iLine, "iVal == DEBUG_FILL_WORD");
    return (TRUE);
```

```
    }

    // See whether you need to check min/max
    // If both are 0, don't check them
    if ((! iMin) && (! iMax))
      return (FALSE);

    // Check against min/max
    if ((iMin <= iVal) && (iVal <= iMax))
      return (FALSE);
    // Nope - tell the user
    AssertPrintf (pFile, iLine, "int should be: %d <= %d <= %d",
                  iMin, iVal, iMax);
    return (TRUE);
}
```

The example shown above will work for most basic uses of an int. If your use for an int is to index into a dynamically allocated array, use the array size as the max when asserting it. No rule says the max has to be a constant.

This example gives you a method of performing boundary checking on an array, but that isn't the important point. The important point is that you can assert something as simple as an int.

AssertStr

Now, let's look at a string. Strings are generally either literals (in which case, you do know their contents and don't need an assert) or are placed in scratch buffers (some of which are malloc'ed). You know some things about a string. First of all, if it is a text string, all the characters are in the range 0x20—0xFE for the English character set. (If you are NLS-aware, there is still a subset of the full character set that will be allowed in most strings. For DBCS, you can also test to be sure all lead bytes have a legitimate second byte.) For this assertion, you also allow the \n character. Any text string in English should pass this assert.

You probably also know the maximum length of the buffer. If you are storing the string in a global or local array, you know the size of the array. If you allocated a buffer, you can get the size of that buffer. Use the following rules for the length of the buffer that you pass to the assert function:

- If the length is the size of the buffer, the longest string is one byte shorter.
- If the length is -1, it's a malloc'ed pointer, and you ask the heap manager for the length of the buffer.
- If the length is zero, you don't know the maximum length, and you don't test for it.

If you know the size of the buffer, you can also fill the unused space after the termination \0 with the fill byte (normally 0xFE). Then, if the termination \0 is overwritten or you skip past it in your logic, you will be reading some very abnormal characters. To assert this, however, you must initialize all strings this way.

Again, this provides a powerful tool for verifying a string. Although it will not differentiate between the right and wrong string, it will differentiate between a pointer to a string and a pointer to most data structures.

Assert a Structure

For structures, assert falls into two parts. The first part is to determine if you are pointing at a structure. To check this, if **DEBUG** is defined, place an unsigned int (I named it "uID") as the last element of every struct of importance.

Then, whenever you have initialized the struct, set uID to a specific ID value. (Use a different value for each struct.) When you are finished with the structure, set uID to a specific "done" value; this can be the same for all of the structs. In C++, this is trivial; set uID to the struct-specific ID value in the constructor and set it to the done value in the destructor.

If you want to get really fancy, you can also put a 32-bit ID at the beginning of each structure. For its ID, use a value that will be the ASCII value for a four-byte abbreviation of the structure (Window = "Win "). That way, when you **db** a pointer in your debugger, you know what type of structure it was set up to be.

Whenever you assert a struct with an ID, check the ID. If it's good, continue. If it is the done value, you are accessing the struct after you are through with it. If it is any other value, you have garbage data. In either of these bad cases, print a message giving the location of the bad data.

Structure IDs

The program example that follows illustrates the use of a structure ID.

```
// Include file:
#define        ID_DONE        0x1234
#define        ID_C/HARWIN    0x1357
typedef struct S_CHARWIN
  {
  int          iRow;
  int          iCol;
  int          iNr;
  int          iNc;
#ifdef DEBUG
  unsigned     uId;
#endif
  } CHARWIN;

// .c file
CHARWIN *CreateWin (CHARWIN *pWin)
{

#ifdef DEBUG
  pWin->uId = ID_CHARWIN;
#endif

  ...

  AssertWin (pWin);
  return (pWin);
}

DeleteWin (CHARWIN *pWin)
{

#ifdef DEBUG
AssertWin (pWin)
  pWin->uId = ID_DONE;
#endif

  ...
}
```

Once you've checked the uID, you know if you are pointing at your structure. If the structure is part of a global list or array of structures, you may want to verify that this structure is in the list. This can be a time-consuming operation, so you may want to have a separate call to assert the global list/array, and only call that assert when you first get the pointer or after you add a structure.

Note: You need to be careful asserting the list when you assert a structure in the list. Normally, the assertion of the list will assert each structure in the list. However, if they keep calling each other, you will run out of stack space very quickly.

Next, you need to verify the contents of the structure. If the structure is holding inconsistent data, you are in as much trouble as if you were pointing to the wrong memory location. Generally, you will find it easy to verify part of the data and very difficult to verify the rest. If it's easy to code and runs fast, verify it. If it's code that will be slow, don't verify it unless it's something that is likely to trip you up. If the coding is complicated, again, don't code it unless you think it might cause you problems later.

Assert a Structure

The program example below illustrates checking a structure.

```
// include file:
#ifdef DEBUG
#define      AssertWin(p)      CheckWin (__FILE__, __LINE__, p)
#else
#define      AssertWin(p)
#endif


...


#ifdef DEBUG
BOOL CheckWin (char const *pFile, int iLine, CHARWIN *pWin)
{

  // Are you pointing at the structure?
  if (pWin->uId == ID_DONE)
    AssertPrintf (pFile,iLine, "Accessed Window after deleted");
  else
    if (pWin->uId != ID_CHARWIN)
      AssertPrintf (pFile, iLine, "Bad Window Pointer");
  if (pWin->uId != ID_CHARWIN)
    return (TRUE);

  // Are the values ok?
```

```
if (pWin->iRow >= pWin->iNr)
   {
   AssertPrintf (pFile, iLine, "iRow = %d, iNr = %d", pWin->iRow,
                 pWin->iNr);
   return (TRUE);
   }

...

return (FALSE);
}
#endif
```

An important trick in writing asserts is to not do too much. If you skip 100 tests among various asserts, and it turns out later that two of them would have found bugs for you, you are ahead of the game. The main thing you are trying to find out is whether you are pointing at the structure, and the uID element does that for you. The second thing you are looking for is whether the structure contents are consistent, and that is usually an all-or-nothing proposition.

Finally, if you sometimes have the data in a subtly inconsistent state and if you think to test for it, you'll probably find you've already coded for it. A good test is to think through everything you could assert. (This will, many times, remind you of some coding you need to do in the program itself.) Then look at each element you are going to test. If the code that sets up the structure is simple and straightforward, don't worry about it. If the code that acts on it is spread all over the place—check it.

Asserting structures is one of the most powerful tools at your command. It's more important to write a decent assert function for every structure than it is to write an awesome assert function for 90 percent of the structures. And, most important, assert the structure throughout your code. Figure 5-1 is an example of asserting a structure in DOS.

Figure 5-1: Asserting a structure in DOS

```
typedef struct S_STR
     {
     char   sBuf[10];
     int    iLen;
#if DEBUG
     unsigned uID;
#endif
     } STR;

#if DEBUG
#define     STR_ID     0x1234
void CheckStr (STR *pStr, char *pFile, int iLine);
#define     AssertStr(p)          CheckStr (p, __FILE__, __LINE__)
#endif


void main (void)
{
STR Str;

   sDebug.iBox = 1;

   StrCpy (Str.sBuf,
   Str.iLen = 4;
   Str.uID = STR_ID;
   AssertStr (&Str);

   // This is a bug!
   StrCpy (Str.sBuf, "Dave Thielen");
   Str.iLen = 12;
   AssertStr (&Str);
}

void CheckStr (STR *pStr, char *pFile, int iLine)
{

   if (pStr->uID != STR_ID)
      {
      DebugMessageBox ("Bad STR: %s\nFile: %s, Line: %d",
                                pStr->sBuf, pFile, iLine);
      return;
      }
}

C:\SRC\NO-BUGS\STDLIB\MEM\TEST>test
```

Overlaid message box:
```
Bad STR: Dave Thiel?
File: test.c, Line: 33
Press <CR> to continue or ESC to exit
```

Parameter Validation

Parameter validation is a type of assertion. On entry to each function, you assert each parameter you were passed. In this manner, you make sure that all of the passed-in parameters are valid.

If you are writing code that will be called by third parties, you should strongly consider leaving parameter validation in your final product. This is one of the big advantages of Windows 3.1 over Windows 3.0.

Perform full parameter testing at the beginning and end of each function. You don't need to test static functions that are called only from one or two places in one other function. However, for functions that can be called from anywhere, full parameter testing is essential. Start at the very low-level functions. If you have a **NULL** pointer, sooner or later you will probably **memcpy** or **strcpy** to it.

Parameter checking can be more extensive than your first glance might indicate. Obviously, you can assert structs and check pointers for a **NULL**. However, you can also check pointers against parameters passing their length. For instance, on a PC, will the **memcpy** cause either of the pointers to wrap? In Windows, is the pointer a legitimate selector, and is its limit as great as the length that will be accessed? See Figure 5-2 for an example of parameter validation of memcpy in DOS.

If a parameter has a range (for example, a drive identifier), check the parameter against its possible legitimate values. If you are accessing malloc'ed memory, the pointer should be in the heap. If you are freeing or reallocating memory, it should be a pointer to an allocated area in the heap.

Be careful not to overcheck. It is legitimate to call free on a **NULL** pointer. You don't want warning messages popping up for function calls that you consider legitimate. You also don't want to make your code bigger just to avoid calling a function in a way that is benign but nevertheless creates a warning message. The checking should cover all errors and no legitimate calls.

Even if a parameter will almost never legitimately have a certain value, you should not check for it. If you get warnings when your program is okay, you will begin to ignore the warnings—including legitimate ones. (Remember the story of the boy who cried wolf once too often?)

Error checking should always continue into the body of the function. The regular part of the function may then elect to return if some parameters are bad. If you fully implement parameter checking, you will be amazed at the number of bugs that you find instantly—as opposed to finding them after hours or days of debugging.

memcpy.c

The program example below illustrates the use of parameter validation.

```
MemCpy (void *pMemDest, void *pMemSrc, unsigned uNum)
{
```

```
#if DEBUG > 0
   // Note: AssertPtr checks to be sure p to p+num-1 is data
   // that belongs to us. And if its malloc'ed data - that it is
   // all within one malloc'ed block of memory.
   if ((AssertPtr (pMemDest, uNum)) || (AssertPtr (pMemSrc, uNum))
       || (! pMemDest)
     DebugMessageBox ("ERROR: memcpy (%p,%p,%x), pMemDest, pMemSrc,
                       uNum);
#endif

   // Even in non-debug mode we check for copying to NULL
   if (! pMemDest)
     return (NULL);

   // Call the function
   return (memcpy (pMemDest, pMemSrc, uNum));
}
```

Figure 5-2: Parameter validation of memcpy in DOS

```
Microsoft (R) Segmented Executable Linker  Version 5.30
Copyright (C) Microsoft Corp 1984-1992.  All rights reserved.

Object Modules [.obj]: test.obj
Run File [test.exe]: "test.exe" /noi
List File [nul.map]: NUL
Libraries [.lib]: sd_dbg.lib +
Libraries [.lib]: sd_std.lib
Definitions File [nul.def]: ;

C:\SRC\NO-BUGS\STDLIB\MEM\TEST>

C:\SRC\NO-BUGS\STDLI ┌──────────────────────────────────┐
#include "_doslib.h" │ MemCpy (2CFA:0,2CFA:50,5)        │
                     └Press <CR> to continue or ESC to exit┘
main ()
{
        sDebug.iBox = 1;

        MemCpy (NULL, "ABCDEFGH", 5);
}

C:\SRC\NO-BUGS\STDLIB\MEM\TEST>test
```

Assert Everything

You can introduce several types of bugs into your code. The easiest to fix are the bugs that stop the compiler from compiling—you are guaranteed to have them fixed before the program runs. (Oh, if only all bug fixes were this self-enforcing!)

At the other extreme are the *do-what-I-say-not-what-I-mean* bugs. Here, logic errors are hard to find because the program is, quite properly, doing exactly what you told it to do. This is where asserts shine. Ideally, your asserts assert what you mean, in addition to what you said.

To handle logic errors, you need to assert everywhere. All return values from a function should be asserted just before return. If you don't know if a function asserts its return values, assert them after calling the function. All functions need to assert all parameters they are passed. If you don't know if the function you are calling asserts, assert just before calling the function.

When you have complicated logic, especially in large loops (or for loops with a lot of code in them), place asserts at the major logic breaks in the loop, including the start of the loop. The asserts at this point should assert everything possible. Do not assert just individual pointers, assert the relationship between them. (For example, if a loop will advance a pointer by two bytes in a string on each iteration, be sure that there are at least two more characters in the string.)

It is critical that the asserts make you confident that you are working with the correct data. You still have to verify that you are performing the correct operations on the data, but you shouldn't have to worry about whether the data itself is correct. Even more important, you shouldn't have to worry about whether your different variables are consistent among themselves. (For example, if p is supposed to be equal to &a[i], **assert (p == &a[i])**.)

If you make liberal use of asserts while you are first writing your code, you will be pleasantly surprised at how much easier they make your coding. The asserts will point you right at many of the bugs you have to fix to get your code running in the first place—bugs that previously took days to find. Generally, time spent writing asserts will pay for itself within a day or two.

Chapter 6

Debug Printfs

We've now written several routines to help us find and eliminate MFUs. However, we need some way for this code to communicate with us. At the same time, we don't want our debug output getting mixed up with our regular output. Therefore, we need debug functions that display information separately.

An effective set of debug printfs makes the difference between the debug information helping you debug or getting in your way. This chapter shows how to display the debug information without letting it interfere with the normal display of data in the program.

You need debug printfs for two reasons. First, you need them for Message Boxes that alert the user to an error, and then stay up until the user presses a key before continuing. Generally, when an assertion or parameter check fails, a Message Box should be used so the user stops at the error.

Second, you need debug printfs for informational messages. These messages tell you what the program is presently doing. The program should continue, without user intervention, after printing each message. Listing the Windows message presently being processed is a good example of an informational message.

The debug printf is an important tool for eliminating bugs in your code. When something is wrong, you should display the error as prominently as possible. A Message Box that pops up in front of the user fulfills this need nicely. Creating a function that makes this pop-up box easy to format and call is important to ensure that it is used wherever and whenever it should be.

However, just as important is a clean and easy way to list the informational debug messages. If properly implemented, these messages let you compare what the program is doing internally to what the monitor says it is doing. If the debug printfs say you are editing one document when your program is showing another, something is probably wrong.

Rather than writing debug printfs to a serial terminal, the program in Appendix B writes to the monochrome monitor, which is divided into a number of windows. Because the monitor is divided into windows, printfs to one window will not scroll valuable information contained in another window off screen.

Conditional debug printfs print only when turned on. They can be turned on and off either with compile-time defines or run-time variables. Using defines is a lot simpler but requires that you rebuild a program to turn some debug printfs on or off. Using debug variables is a little more complicated but allows you to turn debugs on and off without rebuilding the program.

This chapter discusses these three processes: debug pop-up Message Boxes, debug printfs to a second monitor, and conditional debug printfs. Virtually all the code for these functions is listed in Appendices A and B.

Message Box

Even under Windows, a good Message Box function requires some coding; in the case of DOS, it requires quite a bit of work. There are two Message Box functions you can use: DebugMessageBox and DebugMessageRes. DebugMessageBox has the same parameters as printf. DebugMessageRes has a resource number instead of a format string.

The DebugMessageRes resource number moves the format string out of the default data segment. If you make extensive use of assertions and parameter checking (as you should), you may find that the format strings for calls to DebugMessageBox consume a significant percentage of the default data segment, and may cause you to run out of room. Because the job of the debugging code is to fix problems, not to cause them, you should store the strings as resources, rather than as data.

DOS, unlike Windows, does not have resources; in DOS, the strings are stored in a far data segment along with their resource number. When DebugMessageRes is called, the string is copied from the far data segment into a buffer, and then DebugMessageBox is called. This way, the strings are not in the default data segment.

DOS has two types of Message Boxes. The first performs printfs to the screen. The second pops up a box on the screen, and after the user presses a key, the box disappears. What was under the box remains on the screen. The pop-up box will force the screen into 80 x 25 mode before displaying the box, and then place the screen back into its previous mode when done. Therefore, even if your program is not in character mode, if it uses the ROM BIOS to do its screen mode switching, the pop-up box should work fine.

When the box comes up, you may press only **<CR>** or **ESC**. If you press **<CR>**, the program will continue. If you press **ESC**, the program will exit to DOS, leaving the Message Box on the screen. **ESC** is useful if you run into an error that makes you want to bail out; for instance, when continuing might result in reformatting your hard disk. **ESC** has the added benefit of leaving the debug message on the screen. For an example of DebugMessageBox used in DOS, see Figure 6-1 on the following page.

Windows uses the Windows MessageBox function (see Figure 6-2). It is brought up in a TASKMODAL state so your Windows program is stopped, but you can still use other programs on the system. Because exiting a Windows application causes numerous messages to be handled, pressing **ESC** in Windows does not exit the program. Instead, it turns off the DebugMessageBox processing, so subsequent messages are not displayed.

This demonstrates a difference in the way DOS and Windows function. I have found that under Windows, it is common for one error to generate dozens of error messages. Yet, I might want to continue testing, after the first error occurs, without having to press **<CR>** 100 times. Under DOS, this cascading of errors is a lot less common. This is the nature of the differences between the two environments.

Debug messages can be printed one other way. Using the DebugPrintf described later in this chapter, the debug message displays in Window 3 of the debug monitor, and then waits for a key press. Using this system, the program display is not affected at all.

Figure 6-1: Using DebugMessageBox in DOS

```
void main()
{
   int Bool;


#if DEBUG > 0
                sDebug.iBox=1;    /* send debug output to pop-up box */
                DebugMessageBox(__FILE__,__LINE__,"This is a test");
                sDebug.iBox=0;   /* send debug back to debug monitor */
#endif
                ┌═ERROR - FILE dostest.c:LINE 14═┐
                │ This is a test                 │
         /* This one Press <CR> to continue or ESC to exit
   Bool=0;
   sDebug.iBox=1;   /*debug output to pop-up box*/
   AssertBool(Bool);
         /* This one should fail */
   Bool=3;
   AssertBool(Bool);
         /* Parameter Validation Test */
   MemC^C
```

C:\SRC\DISK\TEST1>dostest

Figure 6-2:Using DebugMessageBox in Windows

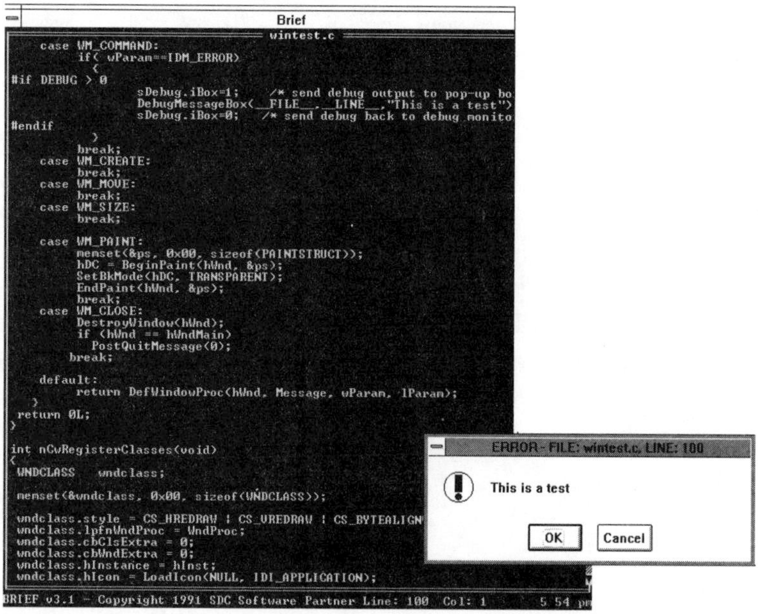

Debug Printf

When you're writing a program, even when you're not looking for bugs, it's sometimes very useful to be able to print out information on the internal state of the system. However, you do not want to print this information on your main screen because it will interfere with the program you are running.

Fortunately, most color video cards can coexist in your system with a monochrome card. You can write to this second monitor, and the debug **printfs** will not interfere with the main screen display. Also, since the printfs go directly to video memory, they don't affect DOS.

Divide the monitor into several different fixed-size/location windows, and write a printf in which the first parameter is an int that states which window to write to. You can then write information to the second monitor.

The purpose of multiple windows is to protect important information from being scrolled off the screen by subsequent, possibly unimportant information. In Windows, I have one window that lists messages sent to my **WndProcs**, and one just for debug/error messages. This leaves me three windows for printing other messages of varying importance.

Because of this second screen, I rarely use Code View. Generally, all of the information I need to know is listed on the second monitor. I have also used this method in writing DOS programs. The main drawback is that when the debugger comes up, it overwrites the information on the second screen.

The enclosed code allows any number of windows to be defined at compile time. The MDA (Monochrome Display Adapter) code is all in **mda.c** (see Appendix B), so it is very easy to write a driver that sends the debug **printfs** to a serial terminal or other monitor.

Along with writing to multiple windows, a number of other functions are available. Whenever the MDA is being written to, pressing **SCROLL LOCK** (**NUM LOCK** under Windows, because **SCROLL LOCK** is not updated by Windows at interrupt time) will cause the printf to pause. At that point, by using the various shift keys, you can stop certain debug functions. Writing to Monochrone Display is shown in Figure 6-3 on the following page.

By pressing the right shift key, you can have the MDA dumped to the printer when the **printf** is paused. When the key is pressed, the contents of the monitor are dumped to LPT1 (with the full IBM character set, or just ASCII).

Figure 6-3: Writing to Monochrome Display

```
>                                              0,112,159])
CreateWindow (Hb17,Spread Win - 14 x 6,[160,35,29 W2(13956,E-QText: (0<79)->0)
9,218](35,160,183,139),...)                    W0(13956,Paint: 13956,3190,[0,
_WinCreate (12,List Win - with hdr & ftr - 20 ite 0,96,159])
ms,[240,315,352,490],...)                       W2(13560,E-QText: (0<79)->0)
Before _HbWinPos ([240,315,352,490](315,240,175,1 W0(13560,Paint: 13560,3166,[0,
12))                                            0,72,230])
After _HbWinPos ([240,315,379,498](315,240,183,13 W1(13560,E-QText: (0<79)->0)
9))                                             W0(13560,Activate: OFF (Old: 4
CreateWindow (Hb12,List Win - with hdr & ftr - 20 748))
  items,[240,315,379,498](315,240,183,139),...) W0(14256,Activate: OFF (Old: -
1                                               1))
                                                W0(13956,Activate: OFF (Old: -
                                                1))
                                                W0(13560,Activate: OFF (Old: -
                                                1))
                                                W0(12432,Activate: OFF (Old: -
                                                1))
                                                W0(13560,Focus: OFF (New: 4748
                                                ))
2                             3                 
Hobbes: 0.909 (3.10)3_3P     Starting: (4462,0)  W0(14256,¿: 33 (0,0))
                             Calling HbMsgStart   W0(13956,¿: 33 (0,0))
                             Starting the loop    W0(13560,¿: 33 (0,0))
Written by: Dave Thielen                         W0(12432,¿: 33 (0,0))
```

The call **DebugPause** will pause until you turn **SCROLL LOCK** (**NUM LOCK** under Windows) on and then off. This gives you an easy way to have the program stop at a given point. This call is used by DebugMessageBox when it prints to Window 3 on the MDA.

I divide the MDA into five windows (0 through 4). Under Windows, I use Window 4 to display the messages being sent to my application. Window 3 is for error messages. (I prefer this to using MessageBox.) Window 2, due to its small size, displays the program's basic state. Window 1 lists important information, and I try to keep this to a minimum so that nothing that's still pertinint scrolls off of this screen due to subsequent **printfs**. Window 0 is for all my other debug **printfs**.

When set up properly (including **DebugPrintfs** at the correct places in your code), it's amazing how valuable this arrangement becomes. When you discover something is wrong, you can generally determine that it is wrong by looking at the contents of the MDA.

Even more important, watching the contents of the MDA while the program runs can alert you to errors that you otherwise might miss. Essentially, the MDA allows you to see the program operating internally in real time.

Conditional Printfs

Once you have added an assert, **DebugPrintf** (and the features discussed preceding), don't remove it from your program. You never know when you might need to use these checks again. Also, removing them is extra work. Instead, use a method to turn the debug code on and off.

You can accomplish this in either of two ways. You can use **#if**s to decide which debug code to compile, or you can use debug variables to determine, at run time, which debug code to execute.

If you are going to be recompiling to change which debugs are on, and you have a very simple set of rules for which debug code you want to execute, use **#if**. If the compile is more complicated, use variables. Both methods are described below.

Conditional Defines

Generally, when I have code where I'm going to use conditional defines, I define two values, **DEBUG** and **VERBOSE**. **DEBUG** sets the amount of error checking I want to perform, and **VERBOSE** sets the amount of information I want sent to the MDA.

While error checking can take some time, it may be as simple as seeing whether a pointer is NULL or if a structure's ID is correct. Neither of these checks takes much time or space.

On the other hand, performing a CRC on all the buffers in a cache is very expensive in terms of time, especially if the function that includes the check is called often. Therefore, as the value of **DEBUG** is increased, the program slows down proportionally. I suggest the following values:

```
DEBUG == 0   No debugging
DEBUG == 1   Left in beta release
DEBUG == 2   Fast checking
DEBUG == 3   Moderate checking
DEBUG == 4   Slow checking
DEBUG == 5   Extremely slow checking
```

For your first beta release, you therefore compile with **-DDEBUG=1**. In return for a slight performance slowdown, your assertions, parameter checks, and so on, will be checked by your beta testers.

This does not mean that you use all of these values for most code. In most debugging code, the checking will be fast, so you perform the checking if **DEBUG > 0**.

If you use this method, be sure that if **DEBUG == 0**, none of the debugging code will be compiled.

Separate from testing is the issue of how much information you want sent to the MDA. If you have a problem with one module, you don't want its **DebugPrintf**s buried in **DebugPrintf**s from other modules that are working properly. The **VERBOSE** define is used to determine which **DebugPrintf**s to use. I suggest the following values:

```
VERBOSE == 0    No DebugPrintfs
VERBOSE == 1    Left in beta release
VERBOSE == 2    No printfs in normal code path
VERBOSE == 3    Very basic printfs
VERBOSE == 4    Moderate printfs
VERBOSE == 5    Verbose printfs
```

Using Variables

The other alternative is to use variables. This method gives you some advantages, such as:

- You can change the variables at run time.
- You can run with different testing without first recompiling the program.
- You can turn levels of debugging on and off while the program is running with your debugger.
- You can turn types of debugging on and off, rather than being limited to a level.

The best method I have seen is simple, yet powerful. Begin with two variables, **BugTyp** and **BugLev**. **BugTyp** is a byte that defines the part of the program. Each part of the program has its own separate number. (For example, you can have a different number for each basic function available from a menu in a program.)

BugLev is an array of bitmaps. For each **BugTyp** value, there is a separate **BugLev** bitmap that determines what debugging to turn on. The values in the bitmap are the same for each **BugLev**. If bit zero means turn on parameter checking, that should work regardless of **BugTyp** value.

To determine whether you should perform a debug check, use the value of **BugTyp** for your function, index **BugLev** with **BugTyp**, and check the value of **BugTyp** against the bit that signifies that the check should be performed.

bugcheck.h

The program example below illustrates the use of **BugTyp** and **BugLev**.

```
extern byte   BugLev [MAX_BUG_TYP] ;
#define       BUG_LEV_FATAL        0x01
#define       BUG_LEV_ERROR        0x02
#define       BUG_LEV_INIT         0x04
#define       BUG_LEV_UNUSUAL      0x08
#define       BUG_LEV_BASIC        0x10
#define       BUG_LEV_MODERATE     0x20
#define       BUG_LEV_VERBOSE      0x40
#define       BUG_LEV_MISC         0x80
#define       IfDebug(Typ,Lev)    (BugLev [Typ]   &   Lev)
```

You would normally initialize **BugLev** to 0x03 or 0x0F for each section of your program. You could then turn various checking on or off. The macro **IfDebug** will return TRUE if you should perform debug checking for a given value of **BugTyp** and a given **BUG_LEV_*** bit.

You should almost never remove a **DebugPrintf** or other debug checking. Instead, set the initial value of **BugLev** for that **BugTyp** so that unneeded debug checking and printfs aren't executed. You never know when you might need a specific check or printf again.

Also, be sure you include any code inside **#if DEBUG > 0** so that the code doesn't exist if debugs are turned off.

Debug Check

The program example below illustrates the use of **IfDebug**.

```
#if DEBUG > 0
  if (IfDebug (DEBUG_SEARCH, BUG_LEV_ERROR))
    AssertSearchStr (pSrchStr);
#endif
```

Debug Printf

```
DebugMessageBox (BYTE bBugTyp, BYTE bBugLev, int iWin, BYTE const
*psFrmt, ...)
{

  if (! IfDebug (bBugTyp, bBugLev))
    return (0);

  ...

}
```

Chapter 7

Watching the Stack

Virtually everyone has written a program in which they run out of stack space. How do we tell? The way I used to find out was if I started getting weird errors. If local variables or return addresses were suddenly overwritten, I would increase the stack. If the problem went away, I would consider it solved.

I got tired of using this guess-and-hope approach to setting the stack size. This chapter presents a way to determine what is actually needed, and lets you set a size that will work on systems with TSRs that use more of your stack than your own system. At the same time, you won't waste memory by having a stack bigger than you need.

An allied problem is using uninitialized local variables. All uninitialized global variables are set to zero in C, so in a sense they are initialized. However, local variables start out with random values, making it extremely difficult to repeat bugs based on this problem. In this chapter, we'll discuss a method that initializes all local variables in debug mode. Then, if your code is using a local variable before you set its value, the bug you get will be repeatable.

While the ideas here should work for any stack-based processor, this type of code is very compiler specific. The code shown here is for Microsoft C 7. This same code can be used for Borland C++ 3 if you are compiling for Windows (**-Gw** option). While the stack checking Borland does for DOS programs is, unfortunately, inline code that we cannot edit, there is no reason you can't use the **-Gw** option on DOS code—allowing you to use the samples here.

Stack Space

How much stack space does your program use? This is a crucial consideration for a program. If your program has too small a stack, it will "blow up" at random times, causing various problems. If the stack is too large, you don't get stack problems, but you do restrict memory that could have been put to better use. That 1 or 2K extra stack you never use (sometimes 4 or 8K) can make a big difference when memory gets tight (for example, if **malloc** fails).

So how is the stack size determined for most programs? In most cases, a developer starts out with the default size. If an error results that the developer attributes to stack overflow, the stack size gets increased by an arbitrary amount. Think about it: in the last program you shipped, how much of the stack is used?

Further, stack size is critical for more than just your own program. When a hardware interrupt occurs, the interrupt handler will use your stack. Many TSRs do also. You should have a stack that is big enough so that your program never uses the last 512 bytes of it. This gives you some leeway to run on systems with BIOSs or TSRs that use more stack than your system. A safe number is 512 bytes because DOS has a small stack (256 bytes), and if a TSR uses more than 256 bytes, the TSR will probably crash DOS.

For other than simple, sequential programs, there is no way to measure stack usage under every circumstance. However, you can easily measure it each time you run the program. By watching it under various circumstances, you can get an idea of the overall usage.

Every time you enter a function, you can check the stack to see whether enough remains. If space gets tight, you can use a **DebugMessageBox** to warn that you are out of stack. With the two tools described in this chapter, you can ensure that your stack is not too big, not too small, but just right. (Thank you, Goldilocks!)

Stack tools are very compiler specific. Each compiler has a variable whose value or location allows you to determine the beginning and end of the stack. Each also has a call (which is optionally called at the beginning of each function) to check whether enough stack remains for the local variables in that function. The code shown next works with Microsoft C 7.

You perform this testing with three simple tools. First, when a program starts, you make a call that will fill the unused stack with a specific value. Since the stack grows downward, fill from SS:SP to the base of the stack. By definition, it must be safe to fill from SS:SP downward because SS:SP is used by hardware interrupts.

stckfill.c

The program example below illustrates filling the unused part of the stack.

```
extern unsigned end;

void StackFill (void)
{
unsigned uLen;
BYTE *pStck;

  pStck = (BYTE *) &end;
  uLen = OFF (&uLen) - OFF (pStck) - 256;
  memset (pStck, '$', uLen);
}
```

When the program ends, you make a call to a second function, which starts at the base of the stack and moves up until it finds a value other than the fill value. This is the size of the unused stack. The second function then prints the total stack size—the amount used and the amount unused.

stckused.c

The program example below illustrates determining the stack usage.

```
extern unsigned end, _atopsp;

void StackUsed (void)
{
unsigned uLen, uStckLen;
BYTE *pStck;

  pStck = (BYTE *) &end;
  uStckLen = _atopsp - OFF (pStck);
  for (uLen=0; uLen<uStckLen; uLen++, pStck++)
    if (*pStck != '$')
      break;
  uLen -= 512;

  printf ("Stack size:%d, Unused:%d, Needed:%d\n", uStckLen, uLen,
          uStckLen-uLen);
}
```

Keep a record of the maximum amount of stack used over time. Add 512 bytes to the maximum, and you have the optimum stack size for your program. Keep in mind that debugging code might increase the stack requirements, so do your final tuning with the debug code not compiled.

Uninitialized local variables are a major stack-related problem. They can be very difficult to find, because you won't even see the problem except under special circumstances. In other cases, the bug will appear in random places (for example, writing to where an uninitialized pointer points), making it very difficult to track down.

The call each compiler can place at the beginning of each function knows exactly what part of the stack is allocated to local variables for that function. This function can then initialize all its local variables to a set value.

This makes it doubly easy to find uninitialized local variable bugs. First, the bug will be repeatable. Second, you use a value that should cause a very noticeable error.

The code below is pulled from chkstk.asm in the Microsoft C version 7 start-up code. It is called on entry to each function, with the number of bytes needed for local variables in AX. On exit, it is expected to have adjusted SP to make room for the local variables, with SP pointing to the base of the local variables' memory.

chkstk.asm

The program example below illustrates the use of chkstk.asm. chkstk.asm is the property of Microsoft Corporation and is included here with permission.

```
STACK_FILL EQU 0FEh

DGROUP GROUP _DATA

_DATA SEGMENT public 'DATA'
assume ss: DGROUP
  public   STKHQQ

  extrn    _end:word        ; stack bottom
  STACK_BASE EQU    offset DGROUP:_end + 512
  STKHQQ      dw   STACK_BASE
  Level       db   0
  OverFlowMsg db   "Out of Stack: %d bytes over", 0
_DATA ENDS

_TEXT SEGMENT public 'CODE'
```

```
assume cs:_TEXT
assume ss: DGROUP
        extrn    _DebugMessageBox :near

        public__chkstk, __aNchkstk
        __chkstk proc near
        __aNchkstk:


        pop     dx
        mov     bx, sp          ; bx = current SP
        sub     bx, ax          ; bx = new position
        jc      cs10            ; Error - out of memory

        cmp     bx, STACK_BASE  ; SP - AX : STKHQQ
                                ; (for heap/stack)
        jb      cs10            ;  Error - out of memory

cs20:   mov     sp, bx          ; Set new stack pointer

        push    di              ; We're okay - fill the stack with
        push    es              ; the fill byte
        push    ss
        pop     es
        mov     di, bx
        mov     cx, ax
        mov     al, STACK_FILL
        rep     stosb
        pop     es
        pop     di

        jmp     dx              ; Return to calling program
```

```
; You are out of stack. You print a message and then
; exit. You should not continue, because IRQs can
; totally mess you up if you don't have enough stack. You can
; use DOS to write to the screen because you have not
; taken the extra stack yet. You should be okay.

; Print Error Message including function called from
; because you use the stack to print out warning you have
; to be careful you aren't reentered here.
```

```
cs10:   cmp     Level, 0
        jne     cs20                    ; Reentered
        inc     Level
        sub     bx, STACK_BASE
        neg     bx
        push    bx
        mov     ax, offset DGROUP:OverflowMsg
        push    ax
        call    _DebugMessageBox
        add     sp, 6

        int     3                       ; Pop up the debugger
        mov     ax, 4CFFh
        int     21h                     ; Exit the program.

__chkstk   endp

_TEXT ENDS
   end
```

Be very sure that you remove this code before shipping your final product. Making a call every time you enter any function seriously slows performance. And don't use this function in your retail release to initialize all local variables to zero. It might seem to be an easier solution than finding a bug caused by uninitialized variables, but you never know what else that bug might be doing.

Chapter 8

Watching the Heap

We now come to the infamous heap, which seems to be the root of the most common bugs in C. Even the loose-pointer bugs are generally due to pointers that, at least in theory, are supposed to be pointing to memory in the heap. Fortunately, there are a number of tricks that we can use to make the heap virtually bug proof.

Most programmers have—usually more than once—created a bug by overwriting the heap. Other serious problems include passing a bad value for a malloc'ed pointer and using a pointer after it has been freed. And leaving memory allocated when it's no longer needed is a quick way to exhaust your heap. This chapter will teach you how to watch for overwriting the end (or beginning) of allocated memory.

The code we'll be discussing runs in two modes. The first, debug mode, will cause memory allocations to take longer and use up more space. The second, for your final release, adds no overhead to memory allocation—neither time nor space. Use the debug mode until you have eliminated heap problems, and then switch to non-debug mode.

The Concepts Behind the Code

The code implements four simple concepts:

1. It places special words before and after all malloc'ed memory. If you overwrite or underwrite malloc'ed memory, the value of these special

words will change, and the next time you check them, you will discover the illegal access.

2. It keeps a doubly linked list of the allocations. Every malloc is entered into the list, and every free is removed. This makes it possible to walk the linked list at any time to check or dump all malloc'ed memory.

3. It stores the location (source module filename and line number) of the call that initially malloc'ed or reallocated the heap memory. All of the malloc calls that affect the heap (malloc, realloc, free, and so on) pass in the name of the file they are called from, and the line number in the file. The filename and line number are then stored with the malloc'ed memory that allocated it. Therefore, when a specific malloc'ed entry in the heap is displayed, it is listed with the location of the call that created, resized, or freed it. This makes it very easy to determine where in your code the listed, allocated memory was malloc'ed, reallocated, and freed.

4. At the beginning of every malloc call, the function walks the heap and checks for overwritten or corrupted memory. Because these checks are performed often, you generally know within 10 or 20 lines that your dynamic memory has problems. This makes debugging relatively simple.

Some Details

The functions AllocCheck, AllocList, and AllocDone exist only in the debug mode. Their use makes no sense in non-debug mode, because the debugging information does not exist in that mode.

I have changed the meaning of some of the functions in non-debug mode. Alloc always returns zero initialized memory. If you don't want this to happen, be sure the debug version fills an alloc with ALLOC_CHK3. Realloc will perform a malloc if you pass in a NULL pointer. It also incorporates expand and NODISCARD into the same function.

Because non-debug is different code, you need to test your program with both non-debug and debug code. In the non-debug code, I have left the extra two bytes on the end of each allocation, although they are initialized to zero. This is an attempt to keep to a minimum problems caused by switching between debug and non-debug modes.

Allocate Some Memory

Every time memory is malloc'ed from the heap, some extra memory is also malloc'ed. The actual memory malloc'ed has a copy of the **ALLOC** struct at the beginning, followed by the number of bytes requested, followed by two more bytes. The pointer returned points to the memory, directly following the ALLOC struct so that the program doesn't see the extra memory malloc'ed from the heap.

The ALLOC struct holds several pieces of information. The pointers pPrevAlloc and pNextAlloc insert it into the linked list of allocations. When you perform an **Alloc** (equivalent to a **malloc**), the newest element is inserted at the end of the linked list, with pPrevAlloc pointing to what was previously the last element, and pNextAlloc pointing to the first element (which is actually a fake). When performing an **AllocFree** (equivalent to a **free**), the element is removed from the list, and the elements before and after the removed element are then set to point to each other.

pFileName and iFileLine identify where the allocation was made. This provides a very useful way to refer to a heap element. On any allocation (alloc, realloc, some, or free), the name and line of the calling function will be placed in these variations, giving you the location of the last call for this element. If you request the size of a bad pointer, AllocSize will list the location it was called from, but the location is not placed in the ALLOC struct.

The uSize element holds the size of the allocation, as requested by the calling program. The size does not include the extra bytes holding the ALLOC struct and end bytes. This is done because there is no standard call to get the size of a malloc'ed element, and when a library does have a call to return the size of an alloc, it is generally much slower than using a uSize.

The uId element holds the value ALLOC_ID. If this element does not hold ALLOC_ID, it is assumed that this is not an element in the heap. This stops the debug code from taking a vacation if the heap has been corrupted. When walking the heap, if an element does not have uId set properly, the walk stops. When passed as a pointer, if this element is not ALLOC_ID, it is assumed that the pointer is bad, and the function returns immediately (returning immediately on an error is acceptable behavior because the *entire* function is debug code).

The uChk element holds ALLOC_CHK1 and checks for underwrites. This happens when you write before the beginning of some malloc'ed memory. Following the struct is the user memory, which is followed by another word that holds ALLOC_CHK2. Whenever the heap is walked, the words at the beginning and end are checked for overwrites and underwrites. If your program writes over these words, the program will continue but it leaves the words overwritten.

Alloc.h

The program example below illustrates the use of the ALLOC structure.

```
typedef          unsigned char   BYTE;
typedef          char            FLAG;
#define          Flag(a)          ((FLAG) ((a) ? (true) : (false)))
#define          Not(a)           ((FLAG) ((a) ? (false) : (true)))

#define          ALLOC_ID         0x1234
#define          ALLOC_CHK1       0x5A96
#define          ALLOC_CHK2       0xA569       // follows malloced mem
#define          ALLOC_CHK3       0xEF         // fills freed mem

typedef struct S_ALLOC
        {
        struct S_ALLOC          *pPrevAlloc;   // points to prev alloc
        struct S_ALLOC          *pNextAlloc;   // points to next alloc
        BYTE                    *pFileName;    // points to file
        int                     iFileLine;     // points to line number
        unsigned                uSize;         // size of alloc
        unsigned                uId;           // ALLOC_ID
        unsigned                uChk;          // ALLOC_CHK1
        } ALLOC;

#define          REALLOC_NONE       0x00
#define          REALLOC_NOMOVE     0x01       // don't move to expand
#define          REALLOC_NODISCARD      0x02   // don't discard on fail

#ifdef DEBUG
#define          Alloc(uSize)      _Alloc (uSize,__FILE__,__LINE__)
#define          AllocFree(pBuf)   _AllocFree (pBuf,__FILE__,__LINE__)
...
#else
#define          Alloc(uSize)      _Alloc (uSize)
#define          AllocFree(pBuf)   _AllocFree (pBuf)
#endif

ALLOC _AllocHeap;
```

The function **_AllocChkHeap** will check a specific heap element passed to it; then call **_AllocHeapWalk** to check the entire heap. **_AllocChkHeap** is called at the beginning of every alloc function that is passed a pointer.

The function **_AllocHeapWalk** checks the entire heap. If it finds an element that has an invalid value for uId, it prints a message, and then exits immediately. (You might prefer to abort rather than return here.) It then checks for overwrites and underwrites on each element, and prints a message if it finds one. If **fShowOk** is true, it will also print out all good allocations.

These functions should never be called in the retail release of the program. Therefore, they should be enclosed within a **#if DEBUG > 0** so they will not be compiled in non-debug mode. If they are called in non-debug mode, a link error will result.

AllocChkHeap and AllocHeapWalk

The program example below illustrates the use of **AllocChkHeap** and **AllocHeap-Walk**.

```
#if DEBUG > 0

// check the item passed and the heap
static FLAG _AllocChkHeap (ALLOC *pAlloc)
{
FLAG fRtn=false;

  // check the alloc on
  if ((pAlloc != NULL) && (pAlloc->uId != ALLOC_ID))
    {
    _AllocPrintf (pAlloc, "Bad Pointer", true);
    fRtn = true;
    }

  if (_AllocWalkHeap (false))
    return (true);
  return (fRtn);
}

// list the heap
static FLAG _AllocWalkHeap (FLAG fShowOk)
{
```

```
BYTE *pStr;
ALLOC *pAlloc;
FLAG fRtn;

  // walk the heap - check ID, begin and end check words
  if ((pAlloc=_AllocHeap.pNextAlloc) == NULL)
    return (false);

  for (fRtn=false; pAlloc!= &_AllocHeap; pAlloc=pAlloc->pNextAlloc)
    {
    if (pAlloc->uId != ALLOC_ID)
      {
      _AllocPrintf (pAlloc, "***** Heap Corrupted", true);
      return (true);
      }
    pStr = NULL;
    if (pAlloc->uChk != ALLOC_CHK1)
      pStr = "Underwrite";
    if ( *((unsigned *) (((BYTE *) pAlloc) + sizeof (ALLOC) +
          pAlloc->uSize)) != ALLOC_CHK2)
      {
      if (pStr)
        pStr = "Under&Overwrite";
      else
        pStr = "Overwrite";
      }
    if (pStr)
      _AllocPrintf (pAlloc, pStr, true);
    else
      if (fShowOk)
        _AllocPrintf (pAlloc, "Ok: ", false);
    }

  return (fRtn);
}

static void _AllocPrintf (ALLOC *pAlloc,BYTE *pStr,FLAG fErr)
{

  if (fErr)
    DebugPrintf ("ERROR Alloc: ");
  if (pAlloc->uId == ALLOC_ID)
```

```
         DebugPrintf ("%s, File: %s, Line:%d, Ptr:%#x, Size:%u\n", pStr,
                     pAlloc->pFileName, pAlloc->iFileLine, pAlloc+1,
                     pAlloc->uSize);
      else
         DebugPrintf ("%s, BAD PTR, Ptr:%#x, Size:%u\n", pStr, pAlloc+1,
                     pAlloc->uSize);
}

#endif
```

Very simply, **Alloc** calls **malloc**, places the new allocation in the linked list, and zeroes out the memory. The ***pAlloc++ = sAlloc** changes the value of pAlloc from the leading struct to the user area of the memory. Notice that after the memset of the user memory, it sets the word value directly after the user memory.

Because we zero memory even in non-debug mode, we need a non-debug version of Alloc. Therefore, we have a very simple, fast Alloc for non-debug mode.

You will notice that _Alloc, as well as numerous other calls in this book, has different parameters in the debug and non-debug versions—specifically, the module name and line number the function was called from. In each case, pFile and iLine are always the last elements, so it is not harmful if debug and non-debug code is mixed (although you may get interesting filenames on a DebugPrintf).

Alloc

The program example below illustrates the use of **Alloc**.

```
#if DEBUG

void *_Alloc (unsigned uSize,BYTE *pFile,int iLine)
{
ALLOC *pAlloc;
ALLOC sAlloc;

   // you need to do this first in case of an error
   _AllocInit (&sAlloc, uSize, pFile, iLine);

   // see if the heap is ok. This takes a while, so don't
   // do it if DEBUG is < 2.
#if DEBUG > 1
   if (_AllocChkHeap (&sAlloc))
```

```
      return (NULL);
#endif

  if (uSize > 0xFFFE-sizeof(ALLOC)-2)
    {
    _AllocPrintf (&sAlloc, "Malloced too much memory", true);
    return (NULL);
    }

  if ((pAlloc = malloc (uSize+sizeof(ALLOC)+2)) == NULL)
    return (NULL);

  // insert it into the linked list
  if (_AllocHeap.pPrevAlloc == NULL)
    {
    sAlloc.pPrevAlloc = &_AllocHeap;
    _AllocHeap.pNextAlloc = pAlloc;
    }
  else
    {
    sAlloc.pPrevAlloc = _AllocHeap.pPrevAlloc;
    (_AllocHeap.pPrevAlloc)->pNextAlloc = pAlloc;
    }
  sAlloc.pNextAlloc = &_AllocHeap;
  _AllocHeap.pPrevAlloc = pAlloc;

  // put the struct contents in
  *pAlloc++ = sAlloc;

  // zero it out and put the chk at the end
  memset (pAlloc, 0, uSize);
  *((unsigned *) (((BYTE *) pAlloc) + uSize)) = ALLOC_CHK2;

  return ((void *) pAlloc);
}

#else

void *_Alloc (unsigned uSize)
{
void *pRtn;
```

```
  if (uSize > 0xFFFE-2)
    return (NULL);

  if (! (pRtn = malloc (uSize+2)))
    return (NULL);

  memset (pRtn, 0, uSize+2);
  return (pRtn);
}

#endif

static void _AllocInit (ALLOC *pAlloc,unsigned uSize,BYTE
*pFile,int iLine)
{

  pAlloc->pFileName = pFile;
  pAlloc->iFileLine = iLine;
  pAlloc->uSize = uSize;
  pAlloc->uId = ALLOC_ID;
  pAlloc->uChk = ALLOC_CHK1;
}
```

When freeing memory, you should double-check the entire list of malloc'ed memory. If the heap is still okay at this point, you did nothing wrong with the pointer you passed in. Now, we'll take this pointer out of the linked list.

Another common heap bug is to free a pointer and then try to access it again. Therefore, we fill the memory before freeing it. This guarantees that accessing the pointer again will return garbage. This step catches any accesses to the freed memory.

AllocFree

The program example below illustrates the use of **AllocFree**.

```
void _AllocFree (void *pMem,BYTE *pFile,int iLine)
{
ALLOC *pAlloc;

  // Doing a free on NULL is NOT an error
  if (! pMem)
    return;
```

```
   // you need to do this first in case of an error
   pAlloc = ((ALLOC *) pMem) - 1;
   pAlloc->pFileName = pFile;
   pAlloc->iFileLine = iLine;

   // see whether the heap is okay. This takes a while, so don't
   // do it if DEBUG is < 2.
#if DEBUG > 1
   if (_AllocChkHeap (&sAlloc))
     return (NULL);
#endif

   // take it out of the list
   if (pAlloc->pPrevAlloc == pAlloc->pNextAlloc)
     _AllocHeap.pPrevAlloc = _AllocHeap.pNextAlloc = NULL;
   else
     {
     (pAlloc->pPrevAlloc)->pNextAlloc = pAlloc->pNextAlloc;
     (pAlloc->pNextAlloc)->pPrevAlloc = pAlloc->pPrevAlloc;
     }

   // fill up the memory in case it's accessed
   memset (pAlloc, ALLOC_CHK3, pAlloc->uSize + sizeof (ALLOC) + 2);

   // free it
   free ((void *) pAlloc);
}
```

Realloc is complicated because of its ability to handle the NOMOVE and NODISCARD flags. If the pointer passed is bad, it returns NULL immediately.

If NOMOVE is not set, it allocates a new element of the new size. It then copies the old element contents to the new element and frees the old element. This always forces a realloc to move, and freeing the old element will trash the contents of the old pointer. Therefore, if you don't use the new pointer from a realloc or access the old pointer after a realloc, you will get bad data. This is purposely designed to cause an immediate and noticeable error if you use an old pointer after a realloc. Otherwise, you might get an intermittent bug on a realloc.

AllocRealloc

The program example below illustrates the use of **Realloc**.

```
// you move it (if it's movable) so if it the program assumes it
// stays - it's hosed
void *_AllocRealloc (void *pMem,unsigned uSize,BYTE bFlags,BYTE
*pFile,int iLine)
{
ALLOC *pAlloc, *pAllocNew;

  if (! pMem)
    return (_Alloc (uSize, pFile, iLine));

  // let's get the struct
  pAlloc = ((ALLOC *) pMem) - 1;

  // Do you have a ptr?
  if (pAlloc->uId != ALLOC_ID)
    {
    DebugPrintf ("ERROR Alloc: AllocRealloc on bad pointer(%#x),
                File:%s, Line:%d\n", pMem, pFile, iLine);
    _AllocChkHeap (NULL);
    return (NULL);
    }

  pAlloc->pFileName = pFile;
  pAlloc->iFileLine = iLine;

  // see whether the heap is okay
  if (_AllocChkHeap (pAlloc))
    return (NULL);

  // can't up it
  if (uSize > 0xFFFE-sizeof(ALLOC)-2)
    {
    _AllocPrintf (pAlloc, "Malloced too much memory", true);
    if (! (bFlags & REALLOC_NODISCARD))
      AllocFree (pMem);
    return (NULL);
    }
```

```
    // let's get the new heap
    if (! (bFlags & REALLOC_NOMOVE))
      {
      if (pAllocNew = _Alloc (uSize, pFile, iLine))
        {
        // copy contents across (no need to zero extra, allocate did it)
        MemCpy (pAllocNew, pMem, Min (uSize, pAlloc->uSize));
        AllocFree (pMem);
        pAllocNew--;
        }
      }
    else
      if ((pAllocNew = _expand (pAlloc, uSize+sizeof(ALLOC)+2)) != NULL)
        {
        if (uSize > pAlloc->uSize)
            MemSet (pAllocNew+sizeof(ALLOC)+pAlloc->uSize, 0, uSize -
                  pAlloc->uSize);
        pAllocNew->pFileName = pFile;
        pAllocNew->iFileLine = iLine;
        }

    // no mem avail
    if (! pAllocNew)
      {
      _AllocPrintf (pAlloc, "No memory avail", true);
      if (! (bFlags & REALLOC_NODISCARD))
        AllocFree (pMem);
      return (NULL);
      }

    return ((void *) (pAllocNew + 1));
}
```

AllocCheck will dump all bad malloc'ed elements. AllocList will dump all malloc'ed elements, good and bad. Their purpose is to assist in debugging, and you can call either at any time. If the heap is getting trashed somewhere and you are not sure exactly where, put in a number of calls to AllocCheck. A message will appear, pinpointing the place where the heap is corrupted. (The corruption will occur after the previous AllocCheck and before the one listing the corruption.)

If you are not freeing up all of your malloc'ed memory at the end of a function in your code, call AllocList before and after your function. With this, you can track down where you are not freeing a pointer.

How to Use the Memory

The following practices will not solve all of your heap problems, but they will take you a long way in that direction. The beauty of this system is that once you start using it, it stays invisible—until you make a mistake. When you do make a mistake in handling your heap, the system will usually tell you exactly where to look for the bug.

Be Sure All Freed

AllocDone should be called at the end of your program. This is a final check to ensure that the heap is not corrupted, and that you have freed up all allocations. Although it's okay to not free a pointer that must remain malloc'ed for the entire life of the program, you should be sure that all pointers used for shorter periods are freed.

I free all pointers that exist for the life of the program before I call AllocDone. That way, if I see *any* elements left in the heap, I know that I forgot to free a pointer somewhere.

AllocDone

The program example below illustrates the use of **AllocDone**.

```
FLAG _AllocDone ()
{

   if (_AllocHeap.pNextAlloc == NULL)
      {
      DebugPrintf ("NO remaining Allocs\n");
      return (false);
      }

   DebugPrintf ("Remaining Allocs:\n");
   if (_AllocWalkHeap (true))
```

```
      DebugPrintf ("ERROR: Alloc Heap Corrupted\n");
   return (true);
}
```

Asserting a Pointer to the Heap

There are times when you will want to assert a pointer that you believe is allocated from the heap and is at least *n* bytes long. Using _AllocChkHeap, you can verify that our pointer is good. Using AllocSize, you can then verify the length.

AssertHeapPtr

```
#if DEBUG > 0
#define      AssertHeapPtr(p,s)        CheckHeapPtr (p, s)
#else
#define      AssertHeapPtr(p,s)
#endif


...


void CheckHeapPtr (void *pMem, unsigned uLen)
{
ALLOC *pAlloc;
unsigned uSize;

  // Get the ALLOC struc
  pAlloc = ((ALLOC *) pMem) - 1;

  // See if its a legit pointer
  if (_AllocChkHeap (pAlloc))
    return;

  // Check its size
  if ((uSize = AllocSize (pMem)) < uLen)
    DebugPrintf ("Pointer from %s:%d, len: %d < required len %d\n",
                 pAlloc->pFileName, pAlloc->iFileLine, uSize, uLen);
}
```

EMS and XMS

EMS and XMS provide very similar functions and are more difficult to check than heap allocations. They are also trickier to use than regular memory. Therefore, you are more likely to make a mistake with them, and it is imperative to check calls to them as thoroughly as possible.

EMS and XMS are becoming less and less important as time goes on. Windows doesn't use them. DOS applications that need lots of memory are now being written as DPMI applications. Only the DPMI server uses XMS, and the application itself doesn't make any XMS calls.

If you don't care about EMS or XMS, read the brief section below on handle tracking (also used in Chapter 9, *Checking File I/O*), and then skip the rest of the chapter. I have included only enough code in the following sections to convey the basic concepts.

Handle Tracking

Unfortunately, you cannot place headers and tails on EMS/XMS memory the way you can on the heap. However, you can still implement most of the checking you have with the heap.

First of all, for each EMS/XMS allocation, allocate a header like the one you use with the heap. This memory is generated with a malloc in regular memory. Use this malloc'ed memory to track usage of EMS and XMS memory (as well as file handles discussed in the next chapter).

These structures hold the handle of the malloc'ed memory. Because each handle is unique, you have one linked list for EMS and another for XMS. This adds a small amount of processing. With heap memory, you know where the structure is when you are passed a pointer. With EMS and XMS, you have to walk the appropriate linked list to find the handle you are passed.

To do this, you create a set of handle calls. The first creates a linked list. Each linked list has a different data size that is used to store the information associated with a given set of handles. (This becomes important when you're using it to store the filename with file handles, which can be 74 bytes long.)

HdlCreate

The program example that follows illustrates allocating memory to go with a handle.

```
typedef struct S_HANDLE_NEXT
        {
        struct S_HANDLE_NEXT *pNext;
        int             iHdl;
        } HANDLE_NEXT;

typedef struct S_HANDLE_HDR
        {
        HANDLE_NEXT     sHdlNext;
        unsigned        uSize;
        } HANDLE_HDR;

HANDLE_HDR *HdlCreate (unsigned uSize)
{
HANDLE_HDR *pHdl;

  if ((pHdl = malloc (sizeof (HANDLE_HDR))) == NULL)
    return (NULL);

  memset (pHdl, 0, sizeof (HANDLE_HDR));
  pHdl->uSize = uSize;
  return (pHdl);
}
```

Once you have created a list, you need to add an element to the list each time you get a handle. You allocate enough memory to hold a HANDLE_NEXT structure and additional uSize bytes. Therefore, for each EMS/XMS allocation, you will have a **malloc**.

Store the handle in HANDLE_NEXT so you can find a structure for a specific handle. The rest of the information is stored in the additional malloc'ed memory that directly follows the HANDLE_NEXT structure. This additional information is used when writing debug printfs to identify the handle.

For both EMS and XMS, you identify the handle by the module and line number where it was created. However, in the case of EMS, you can also give an allocation a name of up to eight bytes long. Because this name is a better identifier, you also track the name for EMS.

(A note on when to call malloc and when to call Alloc: your non-debug code should contain only calls to Alloc. Your debug code, however, should generally call malloc. There are two reasons for this: First, it is very easy to get into recursive loops when debug code calls debug code. Second, the debug code should make a minimal impact on the system—and every byte counts when it comes to malloc.)

HdlAdd

The program example below illustrates adding an element to the linked list.

```
typedef struct S_HANDLE_XMS
        {
        BYTE        *pFile;
        int         iLine;
        unsigned    uMaxKb;
        } HANDLE_XMS;

// Add a newly malloced handle to the linked list
void HdlAdd (HANDLE_HDR *pHdlHdr, int iHdl, void *pData)
{
HANDLE_NEXT *pHdlNext;

   // Allocate the memory for a linked-list element
   // If you can't get the memory, you simply don't do it
   if ((pHdlNext = malloc (sizeof (HANDLE_NEXT) + pHdlHdr->uSize))
       == NULL)
     return;

   // Add ourselves to the linked list - at the front
   pHdlNext->pNext = pHdlHdr->sHdlNext.pNext;
   pHdlHdr->sHdlNext.pNext = pHdlNext;
   pHdlNext->iHdl = iHdl;

   // If you store additional data, save it
   if (pHdlHdr->uSize)
     memcpy (pHdlNext + 1, pData, pHdlHdr->uSize);
}
```

You can now verify the handle passed to all EMS and XMS functions. If a bad handle is passed, a Message Box will pop up to display the bug.

Because EMS and XMS handles are global to the system instead of to an application, a bad handle can work—but you are using memory belonging to another application. This can lead to intermittent and deadly bugs.

You can also check the function parameters against the size of the malloc'ed memory. This is useful for the copy functions under both EMS and XMS, and it can also be used for the mapping command under EMS.

The HdlFind call allows you to find a linked-list element based on its handle value. This call gives you the functionality you need to verify a handle and retrieve the size of a handle's memory block.

HdlFind

The program example below illustrates HdlFind.

```
void *HdlFind (HANDLE_HDR *pHdlHdr, int iHdl)
{
HANDLE_NEXT *pHdlOn, *pHdlPrev;

  pHdlPrev = &(pHdlHdr->sHdlNext);

  while ((pHdlOn = pHdlPrev->pNext) != NULL)
    {
    // If you find it - return the associated data
    if (pHdlOn->iHdl == iHdl)
      return (pHdlOn + 1);

    pHdlPrev = pHdlOn;
    }

  return (NULL);
}
```

To verify a handle, all you have to do is see whether HdlFind returns a non-NULL value. At the beginning of each EMS and XMS function, you merely add the following code segment:

HdlExist

The program example below illustrates the use of HdlFind in determining whether a passed-in handle is legitimate.

```
#if DEBUG
  if (! HdlFind (pHdlHdrEms, iHdl))
    DebugMessageBox ("func (%d, ...)\nBad Handle", iHdl);
#endif
```

When you free a handle, you need to do the same in your linked list. You do this with HdlDelete. It removes the element from the linked list and then frees the malloc'ed memory. It has to walk the list because you have a singly linked list. You must have the element that comes before the one you want to delete so you can remove the correct element from the linked list.

HdlDelete

The program example below illustrates HdlDelete.

```
void HdlDelete (HANDLE_HDR *pHdlHdr, int iHdl)
{
HANDLE_NEXT *pHdlOn, *pHdlPrev;

  pHdlPrev = &(pHdlHdr->sHdlNext);

  while ((pHdlOn = pHdlPrev->pNext) != NULL)
    {
    // If found, remove it, free it, and return
    if (pHdlOn->iHdl == iHdl)
      {
      pHdlPrev->pNext = pHdlOn->pNext;
      free (pHdlOn);
      return;
      }

    pHdlPrev = pHdlOn;
    }
}
```

Finally, you can determine on exit whether you have freed all of your memory. With XMS memory, you can also determine whether the unfreed XMS memory was left locked on exit—a very bad situation. Because you will store the __FILE__ and __LINE__ from each alloc in the linked list, you can display the location of the alloc on any errors.

Because DOS does not clean up EMS and XMS allocations on exit, it is very important that a program free up all malloc'ed EMS and XMS memory on exit. If it doesn't do this, every time the program is run, it will use up additional memory.

HdlNext

The program example below illustrates HdlNext.

```
void *HdlNext (HANDLE_HDR *pHdlHdr, void *pData)
{
HANDLE_NEXT *pHdlOn;

  // If there are no elements, return NULL
  if (! (pHdlOn = pHdlHdr->sHdlNext.pNext))
    return (NULL);
  // If you passed in NULL, it's find first
  if (! pData)
    return (pHdlOn + 1);

  // Get the one you found last time
  // Re-walk because you DON'T trust to be passed a good value
  while ((pHdlOn + 1) != pData)
    if ((pHdlOn = pHdlOn->pNext) == NULL)
      return (NULL);

  // You have the last one. Get pNext - it may be NULL
  if ((pHdlOn = pHdlOn->pNext) == NULL)
    return (NULL);
  return (pHdlOn + 1);
}
```

When a program exits, it can then call HdlNext to walk the list of malloc'ed EMS and XMS memory to see what has not been freed. Do not use this as a way to clean up a final release of a program; this list should *always* be empty when exiting. If it is not, find out where you should be freeing memory and free it.

Expanded Memory (EMS)

On start-up, most programs need to check to see whether they have real EMS memory (including 386 software emulators), or whether they have an 8086-based software emulator. An 8086-based emulator cannot map the same page of EMS memory to two locations in the page frame simultaneously. A hardware or 386-based software emulator can.

To check this, allocate a page, map it to two physical pages, set the memory in one page to a value, and then check it in the other page to see whether it matches. If it does, change it and check again. If it still matches, you can use the memory.

If you only access EMS by using the copy function, this test is unnecessary. You need to perform this test only if you might end up simultaneously mapping the same physical page to two logical pages.

This check, along with checking the EMS-version support (and determining whether EMS memory even exists), should be part of your check to see whether a system has EMS memory. All of this should occur in both debug and non-debug modes.

On initialization, we allocate a four-page EMS block. We then fill these pages with FILL_CHAR. When a page is mapped to -1 (that is, map nothing), we map in the appropriate page from our four-page block. When a new page is mapped in, we check our FILL_CHAR page.

Doing this performs two services. First, if you read from a page after unmapping it, you will get garbage. Second, if you write to a page after unmapping it, you will see the change when you test on the next map call. You also should test each FILL_CHAR page mapped in the **TestAll** function.

When allocating EMS memory, add the EMS handle to your linked list for EMS. In debug mode, you should also include the file and the line the function was called from.

We also initialize the malloc'ed memory to FILL_CHAR. EMS memory is generally recycled—even more so than heap memory—so that reused memory is almost always holding the same values the previous user assigned to it.

You must save and restore the page state, before and after the fill. Otherwise, a call to allocate EMS memory in debug mode will cause the page map to change. This would introduce a bug.

You can also name the EMS memory. If you do so, copy the name into HANDLE-_EMS. Naming is not required, but doing so makes it easier to identify. Naming is a good idea in general because programs such as mem will display the name.

On all the EMS functions to which you've passed a handle, first check to see whether the passed-in handle is one you recognize. If not, pop up a Message Box that says you passed in a bad handle.

EmsCheckHdl

The following program example illustrates checking the EMS handle.

```
#if DEBUG
  // See whether it's our handle
  if ((pHdlEms = HdlFind (pHdlHdrEms, iHdl)) == NULL)
    DebugMessageBox ("func (%d, ...)\nBad Handle", iHdl, ...);
#endif
```

If, after calling the EMS driver, you get an error, pop up a box identifying the error by the function called, the parameters passed in, and the module and line number where the memory was originally malloc'ed. This should make it very easy to determine which EMS memory had the error.

In many cases, you use EMS only as a storage medium. In that case, you should use the copy command. Copying is usually faster than mapping the memory down, performing the copy, and then unmapping. In addition, you can test a copy. Once a page is mapped, the pointer can be used in any manner, including going past the beginning or end of the page.

On an EmsCopy, you should first test to ensure that the source or destination is EMS memory (it's okay if both are EMS). You then need to test the EMS handles to make sure they are handles you malloc'ed, and that the offset-plus-length is within the number of pages you malloc'ed.

If you perform an overlapping copy within one EMS block, even if the copy is successful, you will still receive an error from the EMS manager. If you receive this error, you should check. Don't put the error up if you passed in an overlapped move. After all, if debug pop-ups are false alarms too often, you will start ignoring them.

If you do need to map in pages, you can perform a number of tests. First, if you never need to map in more than two pages at a time, map them into the middle two pages and keep the FILL_CHAR pages at pages zero and three. This will allow you to discover any write that goes over or under the page limits. Second, you can write an AssertEmsPtr. For a given pointer to EMS, you generally know what handle and page it should be pointing to.

In some cases, it might point to one of several contiguous pages. In this case, you can do the following:

1. Ensure that you are pointing to a page from the correct block.

2. Ensure that the logical page you expect to be mapped is in fact mapped to that physical page.

3. Ensure that the pointer is in fact pointing to the physical page or pages you expect it to be pointing to.

AssertEmsPtr

The program example below illustrates AssertEmsPtr.

```
AssertEmsPtr (void *pBuf,int iHdl,int iPhy,int iLog,int iNum)
{
int iPage;

  // See whether it's our handle
  if ((pHdlEms = HdlFind (pHdlHdrEms, iHdl)) == NULL)
    {
    DebugMessageBox ("AssertEmsPtr (%p, %d, %d, %d, %d)\nBad Handle",
                   pBuf, iHdl, iPhy, iLog, iNum);
    return;
    }

  // Do you have this handle mapped?
  for (iPage=0; iPage<iNum; iPage++)
    if ((aPageMap[iPage+iPhy][0] != iHdl) || (aPageMap[iPage+iPhy][0]
        != iLog+iPhy))
      DebugMessageBox ("AssertEmsPtr (%p, %d, %d, %d, %d)\nMalloced \
File: %s, Line: %d, Name: %s\nHandle %d, Logical page %d mapped \
to Physical page %d", pBuf, iHdl, iPhy, iLog, iNum,
pHdlEms->pFile, pHdlEms->iLine, pHdlEms->sName,
aPageMap[iPage+iPhy][0], aPageMap[iPage+iPhy][1], iPage+iPhy);

    // Is the pointer within the pages?
    if ((pBuf < pBase+iPhy*0x4000) || (pBuf >
        pBase+(iPhy+iNum)*0x4000))
      DebugMessageBox ("AssertEmsPtr (%p, %d, %d, %d, %d)\nMalloced \
File: %s, Line: %d, Name: %s\nPointer out of range", pBuf, iHdl,
iPhy, iLog, iNum, pHdlEms->pFile, pHdlEms->iLine, pHdlEms->sName);
}
```

The rest is all straightforward. When you free an EMS handle, remove it from the Hdl-linked list. Then fill it with FILL_CHAR before you free the EMS memory. When reallocating a handle, if it expands, fill the new pages with FILL_CHAR. When your program ends, walk the linked list to identify any memory that was not freed.

A cautionary note: A lot of the EMS drivers, mainly hardware-based ones, have bugs in them. What's worse, these bugs usually crop up only in specific cases. (For example, copying 16K plus two bytes that exactly crosses three pages.) Although copy seems to be the function that has the most problems, it's not the only one. If you are chasing a bug that only happens on one system, it might not be your fault (although it's still your problem).

Extended Memory (XMS)

You should only access extended memory by the method described in the XMS specification. There is no excuse for doing it any other way, and you will trip over other programs if you use another method, such as int 15h. Using any other method almost guarantees bugs, in which case you will have systems where your program and another program both use the same extended memory.

On all copies to and from XMS, verify that the number of bytes passed to copy is even. This is a requirement of the XMS specification. However, it is enforced on some XMS handlers, but not on others. Passing in an odd number of bytes will lead to errors on some systems.

If you lock XMS memory, be sure you track locks. Locks can cause XMS memory to become fragmented, which can make it a lot less usable. On an XMS free, you should pop up a box if the memory is still locked. Also, you should, when walking unfreed memory at the end of your program, list whether it is locked.

Chapter 9

File I/O

A write-only program is probably one of the deadliest MFUs in existence. A write-only program is one that can save its data to a file—but then it can't read it back. However, by the time the user realizes the problem, it's usually too late—the data is gone.

Also, just in terms of general bugs, many applications assume that most file operations will succeed. I know of numerous compilers and linkers (names withheld to protect the guilty) that simply bomb out if the RAM disk they are using for a temporary file fills up.

This chapter covers what we can do to try and make our file I/O bug-free. Two checks are particularly powerful: consistency checking of the file, and assertion checking of file records. Unfortunately, these are program-specific checks and, therefore, need to be written on a file-type-by-file-type basis.

Consistency Checks

Most files used by programs are not ASCII files; they are data files of some type. (When a linker makes an .EXE file, at that time, the .EXE file is a data file.) And any data file must obey certain rules.

Sometimes the rules are very simple. For example, a WordStar text file is relatively free form. However, its eighth bit should be set often, and at the first letter of a word.

At other times, the rules are strict and complex. In these cases, it can be easy to tell whether the file is truly of the data type you expect. Even more important, you can determine whether the file is good or corrupted.

Using the rules, you can write a consistency check for a file, which when passed a file handle, checks the file. After each open and before each close, you call this consistency check.

If the check takes too much time, set the **#if DEBUG > 4** so it is used only when the tester is willing to trade off speed for maximum debug checking. Also, if possible, have separate open and close functions for each data type. This makes it easier to include the checks.

This check should be as thorough as possible. If your program gets a bad data file, you don't want to waste time tracking down nonexistent bugs in your code (after all, you have enough real bugs to find). When you create a file, if it writes bad data, the data is probably gone forever.

Assertion

Many of the file types with strict rules are written to one block at a time. Each block may be a different size but, nevertheless holds a record or element in the file structure.

If an element has rules within itself, its structure can be asserted. Write an assertion function for the element just as you do for a data structure stored in memory.

After each read and before each write, assert the data. This ensures that your data is actually being read or written. If you are reading or writing bad data, you are virtually guaranteed to have problems.

If you read in bad data, you know about it before your code has to handle it, and where to look if your program chokes on it. If you write bad data, you know that somewhere in your program you have a bug that has corrupted your data. Without the assertion, you might not see the bug until your program reads the bad data and hits another bug trying to handle the bad data.

Open

The parameter checking on an open call is minimal. You can check to see that the filename is not NULL or empty. It's dangerous to check the name to see whether it's legitimate, because various networks allow unique naming conventions.

More important, you can check the sharing bits set. Certain combinations are illegal. In addition, make sure that the sharing is not set to compatibility mode.

On an open, save the __FILE__, __LINE__, name, and handle returned by a successful open. This way, on subsequent errors, you can fully identify the file by the module name and line number where it was opened, as well as by its own name. This is a lot more valuable than simply saying that handle five has an error.

This information is tracked using the **Hdl___** calls discussed in Chapter 8, *Watching the Heap*. These calls store information associated with a handle in regular memory and recall this information on a per-handle basis.

Two specific errors on an open should be considered normal. These are File Doesn't Exist and File Already Exists. These errors should be considered normal returns, just like a successful open.

For any other error, however, you should pop up a Message Box that lists the filename and the error returned. These other errors are not only rare situations, but also ones that might signal other problems.

If the open does succeed—or fails in one of the normal manners—write the information to the debug monitor. Because file opens are rare events, it's useful to record the open by filename and handle returned.

The example below is for the standard open call. This should be repeated for the create and temporary-file calls. All three should use the same hdl-linked list, because all the other file calls work on files created from any of these three sources.

Open

The program example below illustrates the use of open.

```
typedef struct S_HDL_FILE
    {
    char    *pModule;
    int     iLine;
    char    sFile[76];
    } HDL_FILE;

#if DEBUG
Open (char *pName, unsigned uMode, char *pModule, int iLine)
#else
Open (char *pName, unsigned uMode)
#endif
{
int iHdl;
#if DEBUG
```

```
    HDL_FILE HdlFile;
    #endif

    // Check the parameters. This example assumes uMode is al
    // in DOS function 3Dh
    #if DEBUG
       if ((! pName) || (! *pName) || (uMode & 1100b) || ((uMode & 11b)
           == 11b) || (! (uMode & 01110000b) || ((uMode & 01110000b) >
           01000000b))
         DebugMessageBox ("Open (%s, %#X)\nBad Parameters", pName, uMode);
    #endif

       iHdl = open (pName, uMode);

    // Display the results
    #if DEBUG
       if (iHdl >= 0)
         {
         DebugPrint (0, "Open (%s, %#X) = %d.. ", pName, uMode);

         // Save in out handle table for future use
         HdlFile.pModule = pModule;
         HdlFile.iLine = iLine;
         strncpy (HdlFile.sFile, pFile, 76);
         HdlAdd (pHdrHdlFile, iHdl, &HdlFile);
         }
       else

         // See whether it's a standard error
         if ((errno == 02h) || (errno == 50h))
           DebugPrint (0, "ERROR: %#X,  Open (%s, %#X) = -1..  ", errno,
                      pName, uMode);
         else
           DebugMessageBox (0, "ERROR: %#X\nOpen (%s, %#X) = -1", errno,
                          pName, uMode);
    #endif

       return (iHdl);
    }
```

Check Handle-Based Calls

Virtually every file call except open receives a handle as its first parameter. This handle can be verified to check whether it is a handle you opened. This catches not only I/O to unused file handles, which is usually a benign error, but also I/O to handles that don't belong to you. (For instance, a third-party library you are using may have opened a file. Many third-party libraries perform file I/O. If you access one of their files, you can cause bugs in the third-party library. Therefore, checking file handles in this situation is very important.)

The following code should be placed at the beginning of all handle-based file calls. It will pop up a Message Box if an unknown handle is passed in.

Handle Check

The program example below illustrates the use of HdlFind for file I/O.

```
#if DEBUG
  if (HdlFind (pHdrHdlFile, hFil) == NULL)
    DebugMessageBox ("func (%d, ...)\nUnknown Handle", hFil);
#endif
```

On virtually all file I/O calls, an error is a very rare event, but if one does occur, you want to know about it. It may be legitimate, such as running out of disk space. Even so, you want to verify that the program handled the error condition properly.

If you calculate an offset incorrectly, you may seek past the end of your file. If you create a sharing violation, an I/O will fail. If earlier you wrote over some DOS memory data, unexplained errors can occur.

Therefore, at the end of each file function, add a check to see whether errno is nonzero. If so, pop up a Message Box explaining what happened. You will notice that the pop-up box gives not only the handle of the file, but also its name, the module, and the line of source code the open for the file was called from. This makes it very easy to determine which file contains the error.

Errno Check

The program example below illustrates checking a file handle.

```
#if DEBUG
  if (errno)
```

```
    {
    pHdlFil = HdlFind (pHdrHdlFile, hFil);
    DebugMessageBox ("File: %s, Module %s, Line %d\n func (%d, \
...)\nError: %#X", pHdlFil->sName, pHdlFil->pModule,
pHdlFil->iLine, hFil, ..., errno);
    }
#endif
```

Seek

Seek is interesting. In DOS it merely updates a value in the file table; it does no verification of any kind. If you seek past the end of a file and then close the file, the file does not grow to the new seek position. If you seek past the end of available disk space, no error is returned.

You can check seek in two ways:

1. You can perform no testing on it except for checking the handle. You can check instead on reads and writes to see whether you are going past the end of the file.
2. You can check each seek to see whether it is placing the pointer beyond the end of the file.

Whichever method you choose, you should definitely test to see if you seek past the end of the file. (Being paranoid myself, I place the check in both seek *and* read/write.)

A bug that doesn't cause any technical problems can still adversely affect you. Prodigy took a big public relations hit because its program would write past the end of a file, inserting a lot of old, deleted file data in their file in the process. Then users suspected them of uploading that information to IBM. Prodigy lost customers due to this bug.

Because seek is used to determine the file length, you have to be very careful to ensure you don't call yourself indefinitely (although that is a good way to test the stack-checking code). The approach I use is to get the size of the file, perform the seek, and then get the new position. If the final position is beyond the size of the file, there is an error. This method allows you to avoid handling logic for each type of seek.

Seek

The program example below illustrates testing for access past the end of a file.

```
// To keep it short, the hFil and errno checks are not shown
long Seek (int hFil, long lOffset, short sType)
{
long lRtn;
#if DEBUG
long lPosition, lLength, lNew;

  // Get the size of the file
  lPosition = seek (hFil, 0L, 1);
  lLength = seek (hFil, 0L, 2);
  seek (hFil, lPosition, 0);
#endif

  // Perform the seek
  lRtn = seek (hFil, lOffset, sType);

  // Check the new position
  // Pop up if you went past the end of the file
#if DEBUG
  lPosition = seek (hFil, 0L, 1);
  lNew = seek (hFil, 0L, 2);
  seek (hFil, lPosition, 0);
  if (lNew > lPosition)
    {
    pHdlFil = HdlFind (pHdrHdlFile, hFil);
    DebugMessageBox ("File: %s, Module %s, Line %d\n Seek (%d,%ld,%d) \
= %ld\nPast End of File", pHdlFil->sName, pHdlFil->pModule,
pHdlFil->iLine, hFil, lOffset, sType, lNew);
    }
#endif

  // Return the result
  return (lRtn);
}
```

Read

The most important test you can do on a read is to assert the data read after the read completes. If it's possible to do so, assert each read. The assert is more valuable than all other file tests combined.

That said (and, unfortunately, usually ignored), move ahead to the tests you can make on any read. A read call should include a call to test the handle on entry and a test of errno on completion. You should pop up a Message Bug if errno is any value other than zero. When you read the end of a file, errno is zero, so an error is an unusual event.

You should also check to see whether you are reading past the end of the file. You do not have to put this in read if it is already in seek. However, it's such an easy test that I recommend placing it in read also. If the test is not in seek, it *must* be placed in read.

You should place two additional tests in read. The first fills the read buffer before performing the read. Then, if you assume you received a full block when you read the last partial block, you will obviously be using garbage data. Otherwise, the rest of the block is filled with the remains of the previous read. Usually, the leftover data is close enough to what you expect, and your program doesn't crash.

Also, if a read returns the wrong number of bytes read, your program will see obviously bad data. Although this is never a problem with DOS, networks and disk caches are not quite as reliable. This lets you follow Ronald Reagan's maxim: Trust but verify.

The second test checks the return value. Before doing the actual read, get the present offset and size of the file. If the offset plus the number of bytes read is less than or equal to the length, the return should be equal to the number of bytes requested. Otherwise, the return value should be equal to the number of bytes remaining in the file. The return value from a read is well defined. If the return does not match this expected value for any reason, something is very wrong.

Read

The program example below illustrates reading from a file.

```
// hFil, errno, and seek checks not shown to save space
unsigned Read (int hFil, void *pBuf, unsigned uNum)
{
unsigned uRtn;
#if DEBUG
unsigned uCorrect;
long lPosition, lLength;
```

```
   // Get the size of the file
   lPosition = seek (hFil, OL, 1);
   lLength = seek (hFil, OL, 2);
   seek (hFil, lPosition, 0);

   // Fill the buffer
   memset (pBuf, '$', uNum);
#endif

   uRtn = read (hFil, pBuf, uNum);

#if DEBUG
   // See whether you got the right return value
   uCorrect = (lPosition + uNum > lLength) ? (unsigned)
                                       (lLength - lPosition) : uNum;
   if (uCorrect != uRtn)
     {
     pHdlFil = HdlFind (pHdrHdlFile, hFil);
     DebugMessageBox ("File: %s, Module %s, Line %d\nRead (%d,%P,%d) = \
%d\nShould = %d", pHdlFil->sName, pHdlFil->pModule,
pHdlFil->iLine, hFil, pBuf, uNum, uRtn, uCorrect);
     }
#endif

   // Return it
   return (uRtn);
}
```

Write

As with read, the most important test you can perform on a write is to assert the data being written before calling the write. If it's possible to do so, assert each write. The assert is more valuable than all other tests combined.

As with a read, a write should include a call to test the handle on entry and a test of errno on completion. You should pop up a Message Box if errno is any value other than zero.

Unlike read, a write should always return the number of bytes the write requested. The test after a write is simple: Did everything get written and did you get an error?

In the code below you will notice that two different error conditions produce the same error message. This is okay, because the error should always be obvious. If the error is nonzero, that's our problem. If the error is zero, you will see that you were not able to write everything.

Although an error should occur if the disk fills up, the event still deserves a popup. First of all, filling a disk is a rare event, and you should know when it happens. Second, and more important, many programs never test their code if a disk runs out of space. You should be sure your program handles this situation gracefully.

Write

The program example below illustrates writing to a file.

```
// hFil, errno, and seek checks not shown to save space
// Notice the void const for extra type checking
unsigned Write (int hFil, void const *pBuf, unsigned uNum)
{
unsigned uRtn;

  uRtn = write (hFil, pBuf, uNum);
#if DEBUG
  if ((uRtn != uNum) || (errno))
    {
    pHdlFil = HdlFind (pHdrHdlFile, hFil);
    DebugMessageBox ("File: %s, Module %s, Line %d\nWrite (%d,%P,%d) \
= %d\nError: %#X", pHdlFil->sName, pHdlFil->pModule,
pHdlFil->iLine, hFil, pBuf, uNum, uRtn, errno);
    }
#endif

  return (uRtn);
}
```

Close

Close is quite simple and very important. Close checks to see whether the passed-in handle is legitimate, then it closes the file. After closing the file, close must remove its associated information from the hdl-linked list.

Close

The program example below illustrates closing a file.

```
void Close (int hFil)
{

#if DEBUG
  if (HdlFind (pHdrHdlFile, hFil) == NULL)
    DebugMessageBox ("Close (%d)\nUnknown Handle", hFil);
#endif

  close (hFil);

#if DEBUG
  // Close can return an error!
  if (errno)
    {
    pHdlFil = HdlFind (pHdrHdlFile, hFil);
    DebugMessageBox ("File: %s, Module %s, Line %d\nClose \
(%d)\nError: %#X", pHdlFil->sName, pHdlFil->pModule,
pHdlFil->iLine, hFil, errno);
    }

  // Remove us from the linked list
  HdlDelete (pHdrHdlFile, hFil);
#endif
}
```

Be sure you have closed all of your files. Although an open file is not dangerous (DOS will close it), it might point out code that you thought was executed, but wasn't. Also, file handles are a limited resource, so you should free them up when you are done with them. And once a file is closed, its buffers are flushed and its size updated so it will be fully safe if the machine is booted before the program ends.

In short, leaving files open when you exit is lazy, sloppy, and potentially damaging to your program. (Or, to be technical, its *not* a good idea.) Fortunately, the linked list you have kept for all opened files identifies by name the files still open, making it very easy to determine which files are open.

FilesDone

The program example below illustrates listing the files still open on file exit.

```
// Called at program exit to determine which files are
// still open. you check for both your own and other files.
void FilesDone (void)
{
HDL_FILE *pHdlFile;

  // See which files are left open, and then eliminate storage
  for (pHdlFile = HdlNext (pHdlHdrFile, NULL); pHdlFile != NULL;
       pHdlFile = HdlNext (pHdlHdrFile, pHdlFile))
    DebugPrint (0, "File %s opened in %s at line %d still open",
                pHdlFile->sFileName, pHdlFile->pFile, pHdlFile->iLine);

  // Find open files that you don't have in the list
  for (iNum=5; iNum<256; iNum++)
    if (lseek (iNum, 0L, 0) != -1L)
      if (! HdlFind (pHdlHdrFile, iNum))
          DebugPrint (0, "File handle: %d open..  ", iNum);

  // You need to free up the storage so when you look for
  // unfreed memory, it doesn't show our linked list
  HdlClose (pHdlHdrFile);
}
```

Chapter 10

Special Tricks for C++

All the examples so far have been given in C (or in ASM for some of the stack code). However, we are now entering the brave new world of C++. Like almost everyone else in the PC community, I have only been playing with C++ for the last two years, and it's only within the last six months that the compilers have become good enough to use on commercial code. This chapter, therefore, is a first stab at debugging tricks under C++.

We don't have different tricks we perform under C++. Rather, we have unique ways of implementing the tricks listed previously. However, C++ does make it easier to perform some of the tricks.

Override Global New and Delete

To use the heap allocation tricks for **new** and **delete**, redefine new and delete to your own functions. These functions can then work like the alloc and free calls discussed in Chapter 8, *Watching the Heap*. However, you want to keep these calls separate from the way alloc and free were used in Chapter 8. Global variables are legitimately not destroyed when the program ends—this is not a bug. You also want alloc to call malloc and this new to call the original new (they usually map to the same call, but they don't have to).

In non-debug mode, you should not redefine new and delete: it is much more efficient to call them directly. With C++, put the redefinition code inside **#if DEBUG**, and everything else stays the same.

The main reason to redefine new is to fill the memory with FILL_CHAR. This will:

- Set all the variables and virtual function pointers to an obviously bad value.
- Find cases where you use variables that have not already been set.
- Find places where you use virtual functions for which you never defined a legitimate function. (Yes, the compiler should catch this, but you can out-smart it.)

To catch any accesses to a variable that has been deleted, fill the memory again before actually freeing it. This is a more common error under C++ than accessing a freed pointer under C.

We also have the pre- and post-ID bytes, which catch memory underwrites and overwrites. Over/underwrites are rare in the case of new and delete, because they are for variable rather than generic memory. However, since we have redefined new and delete, we might as well add these.

Because underwriting and overwriting are rare in C++, don't bother to build the linked list of allocations. The linked list is used for two things: to see what is free when you exit (you don't care), and to see whether the heap has been overwritten (incredibly rare). This makes new and delete faster, and the extra data used smaller.

Finally, if the new fails (there is no memory to allocate), put up a Message Box. Under C++, the failure of a new is a much subtler bug than the failure of a malloc. With malloc, you *know* when you call it. However, merely by declaring a variable, you may cause 20 news to be called, half of which could fail.

New and Delete

The program example below illustrates redefining new and delete.

```
#if DEBUG

// Redefine new
void* operator new (size_t size)
{
char *pBuf = ::new (size + 4);

  if (! pBuf)
    {
```

```
    DebugMessageBox ("new (%d) failed\n", size);
    return (NULL);
    }

  // Fill with FILL_CHAR, put in the ID bytes
  memset (pBuf + 2, FILL_CHAR, size);
  *((unsigned *) pBuf) = MEM_CHK1;
  *((unsigned *) (pBuf + size + 2)) = MEM_CHK2;

  // return pointer to data area
  return ((void *) (pBuf + 2));
}

// Redefine delete
void* operator delete (void *pBuf, size_t size)
{

  pbuf = ((char*) pbuf) + 2

  // Check the ID bytes
  if ((*((unsigned *) pBuf) != MEM_CHK1) || (*((unsigned *) (
     (char *)pBuf + size + 2)) != MEM_CHK2))
    DebugMessageBox ("delete (%d) under/overwritten\n%#X-%#X", pBuf,
                    *((unsigned *) pBuf), *((unsigned *) ((char *)
                    pBuf + size + 2)));

  // Fill with FILL_CHAR
  memset (pBuf, FILL_CHAR, size + 4);
}

#endif
```

Constructors and Destructors

In constructors, remember to do the two things described below. (By doing this, C++ automates setting up a structure, something you had to perform explicitly in C.)

1. Set all uninitialized variables to FILL_CHAR. Be careful, because the data in a class is not necessarily contiguous. Little things, such as virtual function addresses, can lurk between variables (usually if the variable is a class). If you overwrite these, you are adding bugs, not

finding them. The easiest way around this is to place all the data in a single structure. Then use memset to fill the structure before you initialize any variables.

2. Add an ID byte (or word) to each class in debug mode. In the constructor, you can then set the ID to a known value, which should be different for each class. Because C++ automatically calls the constructor, you are guaranteed that you have set the ID element.

Note: This string class is designed to illustrate some points—it is *not* designed to be a class you would actually use.

String Constructor

The program example below illustrates the use of a string constructor.

```
#define        STRING_ID   0x13
class string
        {
private:
        struct s_string
                {
                char        str[20];
                char        len;
#if DEBUG
                char        ID;
#endif
                };
        };

string :: string ()
{

#if DEBUG
  memset (&vars, FILL_CHAR, sizeof (s_string));
  ID = STRING_ID;
#endif

  // init the vars
  len = 0;
}
```

In the destructor, you first check the ID to see whether it is still correct. If not, either you have a bad pointer or you overwrote the ID—bad news in either case. Because the destructor is called when each and every variable goes out of scope, you are now checking *every* variable. This is an incredibly powerful tool.

Second, you fill the data structure with FILL_CHAR again. Then, if you are accessing this variable after it has been destroyed, you will get garbage data. You also overwrite ID so that the ID will be incorrect. You specifically overwrite ID separate from the memset just in case FILL_CHAR is equal to the correct ID value.

String Destructor

The program example below illustrates the use of a string destructor.

```
// note - you don't need a destructor in non-debug mode
#if DEBUG
string :: ~string ()
{

  // Be sure ID is okay
  if (ID != STRING_ID)
    DebugMessageBox ("Bad String ID returned");

  memset (&vars, FILL_CHAR, sizeof (s_string));
  ID = ~ STRING_ID;
}
#endif
```

By using these practices for constructors and destructors, you eliminate several types of bugs from all classes. If you ever use an uninitialized variable, you will get a bad value (FILL_CHAR). If you get a wrong pointer to the variable, when you destroy the wrong pointer, you will get a message. If you have overwritten the data, you will also get a message. Finally, if you try to access a variable after it is out of scope, you will get bad data.

We gain all of these powerful capabilities by placing a small amount of code in each and every constructor and destructor. And the performance hit is minimal.

Base Class Assert

Many C++ programmers use a base class from which everything is derived. In debug mode only, add two methods to the base class. The first is an assert function. You can then assert any instance of a class by merely calling **inst.Assert ();**. In non-debug mode, assert should be defined as a NULL function so no code is generated for assert calls.

This places an assert where it belongs, as a part of the class definition. As the class changes, so will its assert, making it very simple to assert any instance.

Base Assert

The program example below illustrates the definition of Assert.

```
class base
      {
      ...

#if DEBUG
      void Assert (void);
      void Dump (void);
#else
      void Assert (void) {};
      void Dump (void) {};
#endif
      }

#if DEBUG
void base::Assert (void)
{

   // This function should never be called
   DebugMessageBox ("No Assert for this class - OhOh");
}
#endif
```

The second method you should add is Dump, which will dump out the contents of the class to the debug monitor. As with assert, this puts dump where it belongs, with the class. It also makes it easy to dump out the contents of an instance of a class.

Base Dump

The program example below illustrates the definition of Dump.

```
#if DEBUG
void base::Dump (void)
{

  // This function should never be called
  DebugPrintf (0, "No Dump for this class - OhOh..  ");
}
#endif
```

For each class, you define these two functions only in debug mode. In non-debug mode, the base class definitions of nothing will be used. If one person designs a class, another developer can then assert or dump it without any knowledge of the class itself.

This brings some of the debugging into the object-oriented world. Just because I am trashing an instance of a class doesn't mean I want or have to know how it works. I simply want to know when it is getting trashed.

We can make our asserts as simple as checking for the ID byte or as complicated as making a consistency check on all the data in the class. The important thing is to have an assert for each class that will at least look for the ID. This will catch places where you aren't pointing at the type of variable you think you're pointing at.

String Assert and Dump

The program example below illustrates a string Assert and Dump method.

```
#if DEBUG
void string::Assert (char *pFile=__FILE__,int iLine=__LINE__)
{

  // Are you even pointing at a string?
  if (ID != STRING_ID)
    {
    DebugMessageBox ("string has wrong ID\nFile: %s, Line: %d",
                    pFile, iLine);
    return;
```

```
    }

  // Check the length
  if ((len < 0) || (len > 20))
    DebugMessageBox("string has len:%d (>20)\nFile:%s, Line:%d", len,
                    pFile, iLine);

  // You could check the contents of the string here
  // If you do, return on an iLen error.
}

void string::Dump (void)
{
char sBuf[22];

  // You need to copy str for the printf
  memcpy (sBuf, str, 20);
  sBuf[len] = 0;

  DebugPrintf (0, "string (%d:%s)..  ", len, sBuf);
}
#endif
```

A Debug Class

When I first decided to write this book, I strongly considered writing all the code samples in C++ instead of in C. C++ is not only the language of the future, but it also helps to eliminate certain classes of bug. Unfortunately, it is not the language of today, so this book uses C to present its concepts.

I also wanted to use C++ because a lot of the concepts in this book belong in a debug class. Traps and IntTests, DebugPrintfs, and DebugMessageBoxes should all be part of the debug class. Then, when you call them, you are calling methods in the class.

There is not room in this book to describe every procedure for both C and C++. However, whenever possible, implement the tricks in this book in C++ instead of in C. An inline C++ method is a much better solution than a **#define**.

Chapter 11

Special Tricks for Assembly Language

This chapter discusses a number of tricks for Assembler. In some cases, I will show how to implement the other tricks mentioned earlier in this book and bring up special points about using those tricks in assembly language. Other tricks, though, are specific to Assembler—they handle bugs that you just won't get in a higher-level language (yes, C is slightly higher level than Assembler).

Trap and IntTest

The Trap and IntTest macros are very easy to implement in assembly language. For every conditional jmp, you place a conditional trap before and an IntTest after the jmp instruction. If the jmp will be taken, the Trap will hit an int 3. If it won't be taken, the IntTest will hit an int 3.

With assembly language, you know that you have exercised every machine instruction. With C and C++, you never know if the optimizer created machine-code–level code paths that were never exercised. This problem doesn't exist with assembly language.

TRAP

The program example below illustrates the use of TRAP and IntTest.

```
; Will hit the int 3 if CARRY is set
TRAPc   macro
local   a
if DEBUG
        jnc     short a
        int     3
a:
endif
        endm

; Will hit the int 3
IntTest macro
if DEBUG
        int     3
endif
        endm

; Will hit the int 3 and go no farther
TRAP    macro
local   a
if DEBUG
a:      int     3
        jmp     short a
else
        jmp     FatalErrorHandler
endif
        endm
```

An equivalent Trap macro needs to be written for each conditional jmp. Using the code shown above, each time you put a jc (jmp if carry) in your code, precede it with a TRAPc and follow it with an IntTest.

In assembly language, it is common practice, when first writing the code, to write code paths you know don't work. For example, on an error you can jc to the error handler, but you haven't written the error-handler code yet. In this situation, you place a Trap until you write code that you believe works. If you hit a Trap, you know that going any farther will cause your program to blow up. Therefore, Trap just keeps jmp'ing to its int 3.

jc Example

The following program example illustrates the use of TRAP and IntTest.

```
        ...
        call    GetBuf      ; Returns CY on error
        TRAPc
        jc      Err         ; Call failed
        IntTest
        ...                 ; Finish function
        ret                 ; Successful

        ; NOTE: Error not written yet
Err:    TRAP
```

BUGBUG

In MASM, you can make **BUGBUG** a macro. A **BUGBUG** gives you the advantage of having each **BUGBUG** optionally print to the screen when compiling. As you get close to your final beta release, you should cause these to print. Like Traps and IntTests, these should all be removed by the final beta test.

BUGBUG Example

The program example below illustrates the use of **BUGBUG** in MASM.

```
BUGBUG              macro    str
if PRNT_BUGBUG
%out BUGBUG: str
endif

        ...

        BUGBUG <"Do we need to fix this?">
```

Checking Registers

When leaving an assembly language function, each of the registers falls into one of four categories.

1. The registers in which you return information. If a function returns an int, usually that value is returned in AX. Often, these return values can be asserted, in which case (as with C) they should be asserted on exit.

2. The registers that the function should have preserved. For example, it's a very rare function that will exit with a value for SS and SP different from that with which it was entered. Be sure these values did not change on return. It is okay if they were changed within the function, as long as they were restored on exit.

    We can check these registers by preserving them on entry and checking them on exit. The following macros use pusha to keep the code example short. Also, they don't check segment registers; that check is not needed in a small model program with no far pointers.

    RegEntry must be the first call in each function. If you access variables on the stack, you need to take the pusha into account when determining offsets into the stack for parameters. The equate STACK_OFF can be added to each offset.

    The only call that should come after the RegCheck call is a ret. You might want to include the ret in RegCheck; I prefer to use it separately. A function with no ret at the end looks strange. RegCheck uses add sp, 16 because you can't restore over those registers that have changed. You check against the registers that were pusha'ed, but you then throw the saved values away.

    These macros will find out whether you are preserving a register, and they will also determine whether you have cleaned up the stack properly. If you have not returned SP to its previous value, none of the checks should pass. Test SP first so that if it fails, you think of the stack frame.

Check Registers

The program example below illustrates CHECK_STACK.

```
if DEBUG
STACK_OFF               EQU     16
else
STACK_OFF               EQU     0
endif
```

```
CHECK_STACK             STRUCT
        csFlags dw
        csBPret dw
        csDI            dw
        csSI            dw
        csBP            dw
        csSP            dw
        csBX            dw
        csDX            dw
        csCX            dw
        csAX            dw   .
CHECK_STACK             ENDS

RegEntry                MACRO
if DEBUG
        pusha
endif
        endm

RegCheck  MACRO     r
if DEBUG
        pushf
        push            bp
        mov             bp, sp
irp reg, <r>

ifidni  <reg>, <sp>
        cmp             sp, [bp + csBP]
        TRAPne
else

; bp is special - you have to use the value on the stack
ifidni  <reg>, <bp>
        push            ax
        mov             ax, [bp + csBPret]
        cmp             ax, [bp + csBP]
        pop             ax
        TRAPne

else
        ; Do the rest of the registers
```

```
          ; including al, ah, ..., dh
          ...
endif

endm
          pop               bp
          popf
          add               sp, 16
endif
          endm

func   proc near
          RegEntry

          ; Get the passed in parameter
          mov               bp, sp
          mov               ax, [bp + STACK_OFF + 2]
          ...

          RegCheck  <di,si,bp,sp>
          ret
func   endp
```

3. The Registers that have random values returned in them. These are used by the function and, depending on the code executed and values determined, hold various values on return. In most functions, CX and DX fall into this category.

   These registers can be dangerous, because there is usually a relationship between their final value and the return value of the function. If DX is usually equal to AX, then if another function uses DX instead of AX, a bug will appear only intermittently.

   To avoid this problem, trash the registers that are used by the function but not restored. Do this with a very simple macro that places a specific value into all the trashed registers. You set this word to variously be zero, 7FFFh, and FFFEh. If you run under all three values, the odds are good that no other function is depending on the return values in the functions.

TrashReg

The program example below illustrates TrashReg.

```
TRASH_WORD          EQU         7F7Fh

TrashReg            MACRO       r
if DEBUG
        irp         reg,        <r>
                    if (type (reg)) EQ 1
                            mov reg, TRASH_WORD SHR 8
                    else
                            mov reg, TRASH_WORD
                    endif
        endm
endif
        endm

func    proc

        ; function body
        ...

        TrashReg    <cx,dx>
        ret
func                endp
```

4. The Registers that will change in a function but always return with a specific value. For example, if you have a function that fills a buffer with zero, AX may always have a value of zero on return.

   These registers should not be trashed. They have a known, constant value on exit. It might even be useful to the calling function to make use of this value. In this case, you need to assert that the register is set to this constant value.

ConstReg

The program example below illustrates ConstReg.

```
ConstReg  MACRO     reg, val
          pushf
```

```
        cmp     reg, val
        TRAPne
        popf
endm
```

Creating Local Variables

Local variables are often a source of errors in assembly language programs. When you add a variable or change its size, you may introduce errors: one of the code paths may not eliminate the new variable from the stack before returning. Another code path may reference the old location of a variable—the location used before the new variable shifted everything in the stack. Finally, you cannot initialize your local variables as you do in C.

These problems can be solved by creating a struct that holds your local variables. Then, for a function, substitute the size of the struct to create room for the local variables. When you return, add the size of the struct. Adding or subtracting local variables will cause no problems because of size change.

Also, set BP to the base of the local variables. You can then use the struct to access all the local variables. This has a few advantages such as:

- If a local variable moves in the structure, you are still accessing it at the right location. You do not need to go through and change all **[bp + 8]** to **[bp + 10]**. **[bp + elem]** will continue to work.

- If you remove a local variable, you will know at assembly time whether you are still using it. When the variable has been removed from the struct, code that is still accessing the element will fail to compile because the element has been removed.

- This ensures type-checking to the size of the variable. The assembler will complain if you try to move from a word-size register to or from a byte-size element in the struct.

- In debug mode, you also fill the local variables with a FILL_CHAR. This lets you catch any use of uninitialized local variables. At the same time, you should check to see whether you have enough stack. Because many assembly language programs set up their stack in their own way, checking for stack under run is not shown here. However, you should add in the stack-checking code.

Local Variables

The program example below illustrates the use of a struct for local variables.

```
CreateLocals    MACRO    size
; Be sure you stay word aligned
.errnz(size and 1)

; Make the stack space
        push    bp
        sub     sp, size
        mov     bp, sp

; Fill it if in debug mode
if DEBUG
        pusha
        push    ss
        pop     es
        mov     di, bp
        mov     cx, size SHR 1      ; Word aligned
        mov     ax, FILL_WORD
        rep     stosw
        popa
endif
endm


FreeLocals      MACRO    size
        add     sp, size
        pop     bp
endm

; Using the macros
LCL_FUNC        STRUCT
        var1    dw
        var2    db
        _fill   db              ; To stay word aligned
LCL_FUNC        ENDS

Func    proc
```

```
        CreateLocals    <size LCL_FUNC>

        ; the function
        ...

        FreeLocals      <size LCL_FUNC>
        ret
Func    endp
```

Wrapping It All Together

All these tricks can get a little confusing. You need to check preserved registers and create and free local variables both on entry and exit of the function. You also need to trash some registers, assert others, and check still others for constant values.

The following stub shows how to order all of this. The local variables have to be created and freed inside the register checking. On exit, you should trash first, lest you check a register you are also trashing. You then do asserts before finally checking the preserved registers.

Complete Function

The program example below illustrates the use of all the assembly-specific tricks.

```
LCL_CF  STRUCT
        cfVar1  dw
        cfVar2  dd
LCLCF   ENDS


CompleteFunc proc

        RegEntry                        ; Save for RegCheck
        CreateLocals    <size LCL_CF> ; Create the local vars

; Body of the function
        ...
        FreeLocals      <size LCL_CF>    ; Free the local vars
```

```
        TrashReg   <bx,dx>              ; Set to TRASH_WORD
        ConstReg   cx, 0              ; Should always return 0
        AssertVar  <ax>               ; Should point to buf
        RegCheck   <di,si,bp,sp>      ; Be sure preserved
        ret                                 ; We're done
CompleteFunc endp
```

Chapter 12

The Testing Process

So you've written the program, and it works. So what comes next? You ship it! Just kidding . . . that was the old method. Chapters 12 and 13 describe the second half of creating a program—the testing process. These chapters are as critical to delivering a good product as the coding process itself.

These chapters describe how your testing process should work. Without these practices, you may be left with a program that looks good but is unusable because of the numerous MFUs still in it. So what is the process?

It's very simple: you now have to find and remove all of the MFUs you put in the code. No matter how good a job you did trying to write bug-free code, you *will* have bugs. Your entire testing process depends on whether you live by that philosophy. If you don't believe in testing as the process of finding MFUs that you have surely put in the code, then you won't find them.

Developers and Testers

Most developers, after writing their code, hope that no bugs will be found. After all, their fun is writing the new code. Tracking down and correcting bugs and making sure no new bugs are introduced into the system is generally a very painful process. Developers get upset when bugs are brought to their attention. Fortunately, the attitudes of the developers aren't what affect a product's robustness—it is the attitude of the testers that has the greatest impact on a product.

If testers have that same attitude, you are guaranteed to ship a buggy product. *Testers must take the approach that if they don't find bugs, they have failed.* If they find bug after bug, they should go home happy, with a bonus in their pockets.

To repeat: the job of the test group is not to certify a product bug-free. The job of the test group is to find all of the MFUs in a product. Every day, testers should strive to find a new approach that will break the product they are testing. A good tester is the ultimate cynic—no matter what a developer does, the tester will find a way to break it.

Testers also verify that the product works as advertised. As the marketing staff sells the upcoming product on the basis of its new features, testers must check that each feature is in the product and that it works as expected.

Warts and All

Bugs exist. The testers' goal is to identify every last one of them. Their job is to give us a complete picture of the program as it presently exists.

You might decide not to fix some of the bugs, but you ought to know of every bug that exists before shipping. If you don't know what bugs are in your code, some nasty ones are almost certain to show up *after* you ship. This leads to the "fix-disk of the week" syndrome, where you ship out a fix disk every week to correct some bug that a user found. This syndrome usually perpetuates itself. As you ship fixes for all of the original bugs, you start getting reports of bugs introduced with the fixes.

Setting Up the Process

Fortunately, it's relatively simple to set up a process to find the bugs in a program. All it takes is time and money. Accept the fact that testing is a cost of developing software, and invest in the process.

This does not mean that you have to invest an unlimited amount of time and money. Just as it is impossible to write bug-free software, it is also impossible to find every last bug. However, you should allocate enough resources to the testing process to give yourself the best chance of finding all significant bugs.

Adding testers toward the end of a project works about as well as adding extra developers at the end of a project—that is, it's usually counterproductive. Testing software requires as much skill as writing software. It requires specific training and knowledge. And above all, it requires time over the entire development process.

Like developing, testing is partially an innate talent. Some people can sit down at a program and, almost just by looking at it, bring up the bugs that cause it to "crash and burn." Others can spend days on it and never find a bug.

Generally, you should allocate testing resources proportionally to development. One tester cannot test for 10 developers. By the same token, one developer can't keep 10 testers busy. The actual ratio of testers to developers varies, but generally, for one to four developers who are busy putting MFUs in the code, you need one tester to find them.

The Plan

Let's set up a scenario. Pretend that the last time you shipped a program you had only one dedicated tester, who, the week before you shipped the program, was assisted in testing the program by everyone in the company. The original program and subsequent bug fixes were so bad that most users were better off before they received the update. Now, management is so desperate—really desperate—that they will even try debugging plans that make sense and cost money. They let you have the resources to create a decent test process.

First, you need to create a testing plan. Although software development occurs best in an unstructured environment, testing requires significant structure and planning. The testing plan must not hold up the development process, it should work with the development process on a day-to-day basis. While developers design and code their basic system, testers should determine how they are going to break the program and try to complete their job as developers finish theirs.

Testers should be brought into the development process at the very beginning, before the first code is released for testing. They need to know what they will be getting so they can be prepared to test it. In the case of a new product (as opposed to an update), testers may very well have to start preparing the same day the developers start designing.

The testing plan determines what, how, and when you will test. It details the process whereby testers will report bugs to developers, developers will fix bugs, and testers will verify that the bugs have been fixed. It includes a list of the tests to be written and the test writers.

First, clarify what the program does and how it will be tested. A program looks different to a tester than it does to a developer. The test plan should provide a basic specification of the program from the tester's point of view and allow the tester to create a list of items to test.

Next, determine the testing methods. This includes figuring out the tools you will test with, including those that might not exist and which you will have to devise. This also covers the operating systems on which you need to test.

Develop criteria by which to judge the product. How do you know when a product has been tested enough so it can be shipped? How do you know whether a bug is serious enough to delay shipping? As the shipping deadline approaches, the pressure become intense to declare all known bugs acceptable and simply ship the program. The only way to avoid this is to come up with reasonable objectives early in the process, before pressure mounts. The approval criteria might change during development, but at least you have a strong baseline to work from.

Automation

When the testers sit down to design their tests, they should concentrate on one thing: automation. If at all possible, every test should be fully automated, providing the program with input and checking its output and flagging the tester only if an error is found.

Often, automating a test takes more time than running the test manually once or twice, or even 50 or 100 times. However, testers should still automate as many tests as possible. Any given test will be run hundreds of times before the product is shipped. If the test is automated, you eliminate the possibility of a tester missing an error, and it becomes very easy to run the tests again and again and again. By the end of the project, the investment in automation will pay off many times over.

There is an even more important reason for automating the tests. Before word processors, a document had to have serious errors before we'd consider retyping it. With the advent of word processors, we think nothing of reprinting a 100-page document to correct a single phrase.

By the same measure, if you want to rerun a series of manual tests, you need to have a very good reason to spend the time and money required. However, to rerunning a series of automated tests requires only that someone start them. In fact, because the testers spent the time writing them, the tests will be run whenever possible.

Every time a change is made to the program, no matter how small and insignificant, you can run the automated tests. Towards the end of a project, when only major bug fixes are allowed, this can become critical.

If the process is done right, testers spend most of their time developing automated tests and very little time actually testing. At the same time, test systems are running almost constantly, performing their tests automatically.

Bug Reporting

The bug-reporting process should also be automated. When a bug is reported, as much information as possible should be conveyed to the appropriate developer.

A program that reports all pertinent information about the system on which the bug was found is a very useful feature. It should have a copy of the system's config.sys and autoexec.bat files, motherboard and ROM-BIOS manufacturer, and so on. It should tell you everything that could be relevant to the bug.

The ability to write information to a log file is another useful feature to include in debugged versions of the program. When a bug is found, the contents of the log file can provide all the needed information. Although this is not an appropriate feature in a final product, it is very valuable in beta programs, especially if it can be turned off (for speed).

The tester needs to recreate the bug before passing it on to the developer. If the bug can't be recreated, there's no way of verifying that it has been fixed.

If the bug occurs on only one system, the tester and developer will both have to use that system. This can be a problem if the system in question is located at a beta site. In that case, if the bug is serious enough, the computer will need to be shipped to the development site.

The developer should inform the tester when a bug has been fixed. A communication channel between them should be automated (electronic mail is great for this). The tester is (or should be) the one who determines whether the bug has really been fixed.

If there is no automated test to find the bug that was fixed, the tester should strongly consider adding it to an existing test or writing a test to check for the bug. If it happened once, it could (and probably will) happen again. This "regression testing," as it is called, can be crucial. Many times, fixing a bug will introduce a new bug. When fixing the new bug, another developer might inadvertently reintroduce the old bug.

The Bug Database

Tracking bugs is as critical as finding them. If a bug is found but never fixed, the program is no better off. If a developer determines, after a week of work, that a bug cannot be fixed, you don't want another developer spending a week rediscovering the same thing. Or if two people report the same bug, you don't want two different developers fixing it. If a bug is fixed and then reappears in another later version, referring to the earlier report should point the developer to the actual bug.

A bug database is more than just another database on a computer. It is part communication program, part process, and part database. It is the means by which bugs are followed. Although a one-person effort can simplify a lot of this, the actual process should still exist. A developer or tester working alone still needs to track bugs.

If at all possible, a single person should watch all bugs entered into the system. This person is the Bug Master, one of the most thankless jobs in the entire development process. Individuals who find bugs should also e-mail (or otherwise communicate) the bug reports to a bug alias.

Every developer and tester on the project should be on this alias and should read all e-mail addressed to it. Often, a developer or tester will know the answer to a bug and can e-mail a response to the sender and Bug Master, thus saving a lot of time.

This bears repeating: the job of the developers is not to wait to be assigned a bug. The job of the developers is to help find all the MFUs they put in the program. Getting a copy of every bug report, even if most of them are discarded after reading the first line or two, is critical to this process.

Although everyone reads the e-mail to the bug alias, the Bug Master is the one who acts on it. He or she enters the bug in the database. This entry should include the name of the developer and tester the bug is assigned to, and should then generate e-mail to them and to the person who reported the bug.

When the bug is assigned, it is also assigned a "severity level." This severity level should be a number within a small range and spell out very clearly how critical the bug is. For example:

Level 1   The program causes catastrophic damage (for example, it formats your hard drive).

Level 2   Some major functionality doesn't work (for example, you can't print).

Level 3   Some minor functionality doesn't work (for example, you can't print to a file on another drive).

Level 4   The program works, but something is wrong (for example, spelling mistake, caps lock key ignored).

Level 5   A design flaw (for example, call printing print instead of type).

Level 6   A suggestion for the future (for example, allow wild cards when specifying files to back up).

Categorizing by severity is important for two reasons. First of all, it helps a developer to prioritize bug fixes. Second, as the ship date approaches, only those bugs assigned to a lower severity level will be fixed. (Because fixing a bug always opens the possibility of introducing a new, and potentially more serious, bug, you need to be very careful as your ship date approaches. Although a product should not be shipped with Level 1 or 2 bugs, a Level 3 bug may be left if it would be dangerous to fix it at the last second.)

You can always change the assigned severity of a bug. However, don't change all bugs from Levels 1 or 2 to Level 3 just so you can ship. Using levels is important to enable management to determine when a product can be shipped.

Once a bug is fixed, the developer should enter details of the fix into the bug database. This step provides a reference that can be used in case the bug ever reappears. It is also useful when someone is trying to fix a similar bug.

The developer then e-mails notice to the tester and Bug Master that the bug has been fixed. At this point the bug is assigned to the tester. It is now the responsibility of the tester to determine whether the bug really has been eliminated. Ideally, while the developer was fixing the bug, the tester was writing an automated test to check for the bug.

If multiple developers are working on the same program, it is usually more efficient to "build" the program every few days and hand that build over to the testers. (A build consists of taking the code everyone has checked in, and creating a version of the program for everyone to use and test.) The testers can then test against this build.

Regular (usually weekly) builds give you two big advantages. First, to see if a bug has been fixed, the tester tests against all the changes made during that time period, not just the one small change made to fix that single bug. Second, an entire suite of automated tests can be run against the new build, allowing the testers to determine whether the bug fix has broken anything else.

Finally, if the tester determines that the bug has been fixed, then he or she e-mails an announcement to the Bug Master and developer. The bug is then marked in the database as having been fixed.

Sometimes a developer determines that a bug cannot be fixed. This decision might be reviewed by management, but if the developer is correct, the bug is then marked in the database as "can't be fixed." In this case, it is even more critical that the bug be fully documented in the database because it will probably be reported again.

Finally, time constraints may not allow some bugs to be fixed. Bugs at Levels 5 and 6 may not be worth the time investment. Even if they are, there might not be enough time left before shipping. In either case, these bugs should be noted as "postponed." The list of bugs that were postponed then becomes part of the proposed feature list for the next version.

Throughout this process, the Bug Master (as well as developers and testers) should periodically check the entire database for duplicate bug reports. Occasionally, the Bug Master will find "open" bugs that have either been resolved or can't be resolved.

All bugs that are assigned are considered open. This is the bug count that matters. (Having 1,000 postponed bugs that are really feature enhancements is not a relevant number. Having 1,000 Level 1 and 2 bugs is a sign of serious problems.) This bug count needs to drop every week. If it gets out of control, your ship date will slip further and further into the future.

Although at certain times the count will climb (for example, shortly after a beta release), it must always be brought back under control. The actual count depends on the severity of the bugs, the number of developers on the project, and the stage of the development.

However, for the parts of the program that are complete, the bug count of serious items should be in the single digits for each developer. At the later stages of the program, it should be less than four. If you have a high bug count, the developers have too high a ratio of MFUs to working code.

Having a lot of code that's full of MFUs is useless. If your other option is a smaller body of working code, you are much better off. If the bug count gets too high, stop new development and concentrate on killing the existing bugs. Do not allow new development until the bug count is brought back down to a reasonable level.

Keep in mind that you cannot drastically change the number of bugs that a developer can fix in a day. If the count keeps moving upward, even in full bug-fix mode, you're screwed, and it's time to cancel the project. If the count moves downward at a relatively constant rate, you can't plan on doubling that rate just because your ship date is approaching.

The Testing Process

The success of your testing process depends on three things:

- Your level of organization
- The expertise of your testers
- The support of your management

With a good testing process, you can deliver good software. Without it, you haven't got a prayer. With each buggy update, fewer of your users will stay with your program, and more will switch to a competitor who does do a good job of testing.

Internal Testing

A program is tested by several groups. The developers themselves do some testing—by running the program to see whether their new feature works, if nothing else. The test team uses both automated and manual tests. And finally, users test the program in a beta test.

Although the testing team is also responsible for managing the beta test, this section discusses the tests performed by the internal testers.

The testers are divided into two groups:

- Those with knowledge of the source code (white-box). These testers look at the source code and, based on the code, design and write test programs that will try to break the program.
- Those with knowledge of the product as a power user (black-box). These testers know nothing about the internal logic of the program. Instead, they design tests based on the knowledge a power user of the program would have.

White-Box Testing

Internal testing is generally the only source of white-box testing of a product. Where the Traps and IntTests made sure that all code was executed, white-box testing ensures that all combinations of code paths are tested.

White-box testing cannot be performed by the developer who wrote the code. Any developer, no matter how good, has blind spots, and after all, it's the developer who put all of those MFUs in there in the first place.

Although white-box testing should exercise the common code paths, this is the least important of its jobs. (If a code path is common, the black-box testing will surely test it.) Instead, testers should exercise code paths that will be used very rarely. Ideally, tests will be written for all possible code paths. However, with a limited amount of time and people, this is usually not possible. In that case, the testers have to decide which code paths to test. There are two basic groups of tests.

First, there are those that test the basic functionality of the program and determine whether the basic system, including all critical paths, works. This is necessary in case the developers have made a change that makes it impossible to test anything because the basic system is "hosed" (another technical term that means you can't do anything with the program).

Second, tests should be written for the code paths you think have the best chance of breaking. This is where the test group has its best opportunity to break a program. Also, in the course of looking for code paths to break, a tester who finds something else wrong can bring it to the attention of the developer. This code review is also a way to find bugs.

Black-Box Testing

Black-box testing is the opposite of white-box testing. It is critical that black-box testers be truly "clean." By clean, I mean that the testers must have no knowledge of the internal code that makes up the program.

In most cases, the best way to ensure that black-box testers are clean is to use nonprogrammers. Even if they see code, nonprogrammers will have no idea of what it means, nor can they learn about the internal logic from a developer.

Black-box tests are designed by a power user. Like the white-box tests, two basic groups should be written. First, the tests of common functionality, which verify that the basic program works. Second, once again, are the uncommon code paths. In black-box testing, there is no way to know which code paths are shakier than others. The best approach is to give an unusual response to prompts.

For example, when prompted for a filename, try one- and eight-character names. Try files that are read-only. Try bad files. Try files that don't exist. In other words, try everything except a normal file.

Testing the uncommon code path is not critical in black-box testing, because the beta test will accomplish much of it. More important is adding tests for bugs found in the beta process.

If you track the initial black-box tests, you will find that some testers wrote tests that all succeeded, some wrote tests that sometimes failed, and some wrote tests that almost always failed. Use the people in this latter group to keep writing tests and have the people in the other groups write tests for bugs reported by beta sites.

Designing the Tests

Tests generally have a longer life span than the code they test. Although a program may be completely rewritten between versions, the user interface may stay constant. Because many tests are written to exercise the user interface, the tests are either still good or else easily modifiable. (For example, when a program is converted to another language [human, not programming], most of the tests are still good, although developers may have to change the actual keystroke input and the text in the results to match the new language. Test routines, like programs, have to be written with an eye on international support.)

In the previous section on the bug database, I mentioned "test suites." A test suite is nothing more than a group of test cases. For example, one suite may consist of the basic functionality tests that determine whether the basic program works; another suite may include all of the printing test cases.

Two test suites can have some crossover in the test cases they use. If possible, a test suite should include other test suites. You should also have a test suite for each basic group, as well as a master suite that includes every test in all of these suites.

A test case is a program composed of a set of test scenarios for one feature in a program. By running a test case, you should exercise the feature with every test written for it. If the test case for opening a file passes, it has passed all of the tests you have written for opening a file. A test case should be as comprehensive as possible—it fully and completely tests one feature.

A test case is made up of test scenarios. Each scenario tests one specific way of exercising the function. Using the example of opening a file, one scenario would pass in a filename that doesn't exist. Another would pass in a file that was bad, and so on. A test scenario should be as simple as possible—it tests only one specific code path.

Logs should be generated for the tests made, and they should report results as clearly and simply as possible. The best logs say no more than that tests have been completed successfully, if there were no errors, and report results of a failure.

A professional test group provides a professional series of test suites. When completed, the automated tests should be a smooth-running product, performing its job well and returning results clearly. The tests should be easy to use and require minimal user interaction.

Running the Tests

The very first test is one designed by the testers and run by the developers themselves. Until the software passes this test, it is not handed over to the testers. Its purpose is not for the developers to do the testers' job but to ensure that after bug fixes, the program still works. Enough of the program's main features need to work well enough to allow the testers to actually do something.

This test comprises cases developed by both the white-box and black-box testers for the main code paths. As more of the program gets working, this initial test may be enlarged. However, at no time should it include capabilities not yet built into the program. The test is not to determine whether something works for the first time but only to ensure that the basic functionality that was previously checked out still works correctly.

To repeat: this test must be completely automated. While a developer is not likely to run a manual test once a week, he or she probably will run a program that reports automatically whether the program is working as expected.

Do this by building the product once a week. Once the product is built and includes everyone's changes, the automated test is then run against the program. If the program passes, it is given to the test group. If it doesn't, the program is fixed by the developer or developers who broke the build.

The process of building the program and running the basic test can be done by a developer, a person dedicated to this function (a builder), or a tester. The program may be built and then delivered to the testers to run the basic test. However, if the basic test fails, the sole job of the developers is to fix it. Until that happens, the developers do not do any other development.

Once the build passes the basic tests, it is turned over to the test group. The testers then run their tests, both automated and manual, on the build. The first tests should be those that test whether bugs that were reported fixed have truly been fixed. If not, the bug is returned to the appropriate developer.

Next, if new features were added, the tests developed for them should be run. Because test programs are written concurrently with development, the programs to test new features should be ready as soon as (or before) new features are completed.

This gives developers immediate feedback on how well they have implemented the new function. Instead of waiting weeks or even months, long after they have forgotten all of the details of the implementation, they get feedback within days.

Finally, the remainder of the tests should be run to ensure that no new bugs were introduced into the program. This is where automated tests really pay off. When a new build is delivered to the testers, all of the old tests are rerun at minimal cost.

Testing Platforms

The testers should be sure they test under actual end-user conditions. If most users have 80286 machines with 640K of RAM, testing exclusively with 50 MHz 80486 systems with 8M of memory will allow a lot of problems to slip through.

It's important to run the full set of tests on least-common-denominator systems. The tests must pass on every system the program might be run on—not only the hardware, but also the software it may run with, including networks, TSRs, and so on.

If you use special monitors, test the program with each. Look for combinations that cause trouble. Look for other software packages that might conflict with yours. Conflicts can come from sources other than TSRs and device drivers. Under Windows, your DOS application might be incompatible with another application that is running in another DOS box at the same time.

Be sure you test with various operating system environments. In DOS, you should test with DOS loaded both low and high. Test your program loaded both low and high in a UMB. You also should test your program in a Windows DOS box, which will catch some illegal memory accesses.

If your product is network-aware it is critical that you test it on several networks. Testing a network program on only one network is a good way to guarantee that it will blow up on every other network out there. Use at least three radically different networks. If you talk to different network APIs, depending on the network, test at least two different networks with each API.

If you are writing a Windows application, be sure it works in both 286 and 386 mode. Test 286 mode on both a 286 and 386. In each case, Windows is significantly different. And if your program can run in real mode, test it in real mode. If it's not important enough to you to test it in real mode, you're not doing your customers any favors by allowing them to run the program in real mode.

As object linking and embedding (OLE) becomes more prevalent in Windows applications, compatibility with other applications will become more important. You will start to see bugs where your program blows up only when it has an OLE connection to application B, and application B starts a dynamic data exchange (DDE) connection with application C.

If you are writing a DOS application, be sure it runs on DOS and under Windows in both 286 and 386 modes. Furthermore, even if your application is not network-aware, be sure it runs well if your system has a network loaded on it, both as a workstation and as a server. These environments can make a big difference to your application.

Work on bringing the system to its knees. A common test for software that uses a network is to have everyone on the net perform the same function at the same time. The real test isn't "Can one user retrieve a record over the net?" It's "Can 200 retrieve a record at the same time?" Or "Can 200 retrieve the same record at the same time?"

Testing, Testing

Testers are essentially superusers—not power users who know the program well, but users who can act like a power user one second and a novice the next. Testers not only ensure that a program works as advertised, they also ensure that it is usable. A bug-free program that is too difficult (or weird) is of no use to anyone.

Testers are also the users' advocates with the developers. They are the ones who will first use the system to see what happens, and the first ones who will notice if the program confuses a user.

Just as the tricks for developers described in the earlier chapters attempt to make bugs immediately apparent, so do the tests. Each time a new build is released for testing, an immediate and thorough test for bugs begins. Reports of any bugs identified are immediately communicated to the developers.

Everything relies on the testers being as good at finding MFUs as the developers were at putting the MFUs in the code in the first place.

The Beta Test

A beta test is not a true test process, nor is it a substitute for any of the other parts of the test process. A beta test, by itself, will not find most of the bugs in a program. (Many companies try to use a beta test instead of a proper internal test program. This does *not* work.)

But . . . a beta test is essential. No matter how good your internal test system is, no matter how talented your testers are, no matter how careful your developers may be, you *will* produce code with bugs that all these internal tests cannot find. And the only way to find those bugs is with a beta test.

Although everyone has a beta test nowadays, many of them are not very effective. So what do you want a beta test to accomplish? You want it to accomplish four critical things:

- Test your program on a diverse set of hardware platforms. Of the 80 million PCs in the world, 79,999,998 are each slightly different from all of the others. (There are two in Iowa that are identical.) A beta test allows you to test your program on a much wider selection of hardware than you could possibly have in-house.

  This diversity is critical. As hard as companies try to use a diverse set of hardware for internal testing, the set is, in fact, remarkably similar. Only by using existing platforms across the United States and the world can you make sure your program will run on any hardware combination.

- Second, test your program while it runs with various other programs. Again, aside from the two PCs in Iowa, each computer in the world runs a set of TSRs, device drivers, and so on, that is slightly different from every other computer in the world.

  Add to this a mix of software products. (Some programs in use are so old, they haven't been updated since the invention of hard drives, networks, or hierarchical file systems. Needless to say, some of these programs have trouble with the concept of 640K of RAM and freak out if they see UMBs.)

  A combination of software can cause a completely safe operation to malfunction on some systems. You might actually have to program around bugs in other programs to solve some of these problems. Only a beta test allows your program to be tested against a truly diverse set of combinations.

■ A beta test allows developers to get feedback on a program. If a feature is difficult to use, beta testers will let you know. If a very important feature is missing, they will let you know. If a feature gets in the way and is not needed, they will let you know.

This gives you a chance to fix things before you ship the product and it is too late to make a change. One missing feature in an otherwise outstanding product can drastically reduce sales. One bad feature can ruin a product's usefulness.

Developers are interested in creating a product and testers are interested in finding bugs, but users are interested in using the product. Beta testers are trying to use the software to solve problems. A well-written, bug-free program is not necessarily usable, and usability problems are as serious as a bug.

■ A small subset of beta testers write programs that interact with your program. These users need an advance copy so they can ship an update to their program when you ship yours.

This holds true for operating systems such as Windows and OS/2. It also holds true for word processors for those dependent on your file structure, for programs that have an API you can talk to, and for Windows applications that support DDE and OLE.

This last group is special for two reasons. First, this is a subset of the entire beta test group. Second, depending on the difficulty of incorporating changes that are necessary because of changes in your program, these people may need to get a copy of your product even before the regular beta test.

When to Beta

The first two reasons to have a beta test have to do with alerting you to bugs due to very subtle influences. Testing for these influences should wait until you are near the end of your development process. If the program changes significantly, these subtle influences will also change. You are not concerned about whether an early build of the program won't work with a certain TSR, only if the final build won't.

The third reason to have a beta test concerns how the program acts as a whole. Generally, the feedback from a beta test will uncover small inconsistencies. Or it will find that some users use the program in different ways or under different circumstances that necessitate changes for those circumstances. Again, a relatively complete product is needed to get this type of feedback, so the beta test should come quite late in the process. Many companies make the mistake of starting the beta early, in hopes of hastening the product's ship date. A beta test will not hasten the ship date (although it might prolong it).

There is no reason to start a beta test early. In fact, there are numerous reasons not to start a beta too early. First of all, even though labeled beta, the quality of the product will influence opinions on the final product. (Microsoft C 7 was labeled as a buggy product due to its early beta state, even though the final product was rock-solid.)

Also, if a beta period lasts long enough, the beta product will start to be considered a released product because all of the opinion makers have been working with it for so long. If the product is still buggy or has bad functionality, the product can fail before it is ever released.

On the flip side, you should not wait too long. Initiating a beta period one week prior to shipping the final product is worse than useless. Not only is it no help, but by telling management you had a beta test (and a beta period is *not* a beta test), they might think the product is ready to ship.

The purpose of the beta test is very simple: developers are even more ingenious at putting MFUs in the program than testers are at finding them (sorry, testers). Those MFUs are in the code—you know they are—and you want to find them.

So how do you decide when to start the beta? The first step is to make yourself self-hosted if possible. If you are writing an operating system, the developers should be running the new operating system first. If you are writing a compiler, the compiler should be compiling itself first. (For nonsystems software, self-hosting is not always possible—how many developers use a spreadsheet?)

Also, you should have an internal alpha release. That way, a group of *users* (not testers), preferably within the company that is developing the product, is actually using the product.

Ideally, these users will say that aside from a few bugs, the new product in its present state is preferable to what they are currently using. Once you reach this point, after you fix the minor bugs that were found, you are at the perfect stage to make your first beta release.

If your alpha testers are not able to use the program, there is nothing to be gained by having a larger beta group that cannot use the program. If the alpha testers are reporting significant bugs, you don't need more people reporting the same bugs.

The best guide as to when to start beta testing is that internal testing should be finding just a minimal number of bugs, and the developers should be able to finish coding within another month or two. In other words, you need to get some bugs reported within the next month, or some people won't have anything to do.

When to Ship

You're ready to ship your final beta when you send out a beta and you don't have to make any changes to any part of the core code that is central to the system.

A development group that does a very good job of writing bug-free code will generally have one to two beta releases. (Operating-system software will usually have more because applications talk to operating systems, and this adds another layer to the puzzle.) However, it's better to have additional betas than to ship a buggy product that customers will return.

All of the beta periods, except the final one, can last for any period of time, although the average is one to two months. If you are still receiving lots of new bug reports for an existing beta, there isn't much need to ship a new one. If you have a radically new version, or if you have fixed a lot of critical bugs, it's probably time to ship another beta.

The final beta period should last a minimum of at least one month and, unless you are getting no reports of bugs, really should be two months. The longer you wait, the more unusual the combinations that your program will be put through out in the field.

If you make final changes that you consider safe but that do touch the core code, you might want to consider shipping a limited beta. Ship copies to those sites that have found the most problems.

You might also want to consider beta testing either through CompuServe or some other bulletin board service. If beta testers can download the beta, there is no cost to you for having some intermediate betas in the course of the test. It's hard to believe, but people will actually take the time to download 8M files just to test a program for you.

Selecting Beta Sites

Another important criterion for beta sites is diversity. Two users with identical computers, software, and habits are no more useful than one. Two radically different users with different systems and software *are* useful.

As the beta progresses, track your beta sites. If a beta site never reports any bugs, it's no use to you, and you shouldn't bother to include it the next time you do a beta. There should be an exception for those beta sites that need advance access to your product to adopt a product of their own. Even if they don't report bugs, they need the beta.

Beta sites that report bug after bug need to be rewarded (with a plaque, if nothing else). If after your final beta, you make a change that "sort of" impacts the core code, you might choose to send a postbeta out to just these sites.

A number of companies seem to want to have a larger beta site program than any other. After a certain number, there is no benefit in gaining additional sites. Pick a number and try very hard not to go over it. For a general-purpose product that sells millions of copies, I see no advantage in having more than 5,000 beta sites. For a vertical market application with 1,000 total customers, 50 beta sites is more than enough (and 20 may be sufficient). Pick the right beta sites: picking 20 people who don't actually use the beta is of no use.

You are looking for quality not quantity. Track the people who report bugs on your existing products. Ask (beg, if necessary) those in the top one or two percent to be beta testers. People who call up with good suggestions for future products should also be beta test sites.

Handling Bug Reports

The success of your beta program rests primarily on three things: who you get as beta testers, how motivated they are to find and report bugs, and how you act on the bugs reported.

When a beta site calls in a bug report, the beta program is actually providing its value. Equally important, during this call the beta tester receives feedback that will encourage or discourage him or her in the future.

When a bug report comes in, a tester needs to check to see whether the same bug has already been reported. If it has not, the tester needs to get enough information to duplicate the bug. An incomplete bug report is of no use.

If the beta tester calls in the bug report or if a tester needs to call the beta site for additional information, the tester must make the beta site feel appreciated. Thank people for finding the bug; don't yell at them and tell them that now you'll have to stay at work all night because of what they found.

Let them know you appreciate their time in testing and reporting the bug. Without this positive feedback, a beta site will probably not report the next bug it finds. Make people feel important, appreciated members of the development team.

The bug then needs to be entered into the bug database and assigned to a developer to be fixed. Special care should be taken at this time to ensure this bug has not already been reported.

You might also want to have a tester reproduce the bug before entering it into the database. Some reported bugs may be from earlier versions—or aren't bugs at all. Others are specific to the user's hardware. In any of these cases, there is no point in having the developer try to fix the bug until it can be reproduced.

When a bug is resolved, let the beta site know it was fixed, and thank them again. If they were the first to report it, let them know that, too. If a beta site thinks you aren't paying attention to their reports, they'll give up. People are amazingly willing to help out by testing programs. However, almost no one is willing to do it if they think they are being ignored.

If you have a user newsletter, publish notice of awards to your top 10 beta sites. If you have a users group meeting, present the beta testers with plaques or find some other way to show your appreciation in front of their peers. Make every user aspire to finding more bugs than any other.

Chapter 13

Shipping the Product

This chapter addresses that most difficult of all questions: when to finally ship the product. It is one of the most critical—if not *the* critical—questions. Ship too soon, and the MFUs in the program will force you to ship fix disks. Ship too late, and someone may beat you to market; at the very least, you've delayed the revenue you may need to survive.

This question is difficult because, even with adequate testing, you will always have some bugs. What you are trying to do is come up with a release that has no bugs serious enough to stop you from shipping the program.

As you get close to completing the final beta version of your software, you build a release candidate. You will ship this copy as the final product—unless a significant bug is found. (Note: If the developers are still working on bug fixes for the program, you are nowhere close to the release candidate stage.)

You should put this release candidate through full regression tests (all of your automated and manual tests). If the software passes the regression tests, everyone on the project, testers and nontesters alike, should try to break the program. They should spend a couple of days doing nothing but beating up on the product.

At this point, you need to send this "mini-beta" release candidate to everyone in the company, as well as to selected beta sites. As I mentioned earlier, send it to the beta sites that have found the most errors in the past. You might also want to put the beta on CompuServe, or another bulletin board, for beta testers to download. It doesn't cost you anything to do this, and it gets you an additional pool of testers. (If you are scared to send it to beta sites because they might find bugs—then again, you are *not* ready to ship it.)

The final test should last at least a week. If you made changes to core parts of the program or to the file structure of its files, this test should last a month. There is simply no way to shorten this period; it takes time for users to manipulate the program in different ways and to exercise unique combinations of the code.

When the program has passed the tests, it is ready for release to the manufacturer. Have your manufacturing department send you the first 10 sets of disks made, and have everyone in your group install the program from the disks and test it again. Be sure that what you sent to manufacturing is what you get back. Comparing the disks isn't good enough; you should be sure the program runs.

To Release or Not To Release

If the release candidate fails any of the regression tests, you must decide whether the bug is a release stopper. Don't forget, fixing a bug can introduce a new, unknown bug. If do you make a change, you need to take the time to repeat the entire test cycle. You need to be totally paranoid, and believe that the fix might have introduced a subtle, and very serious, bug into the program. If the change was in an area of any significance, you need to send the program out to a "mini-beta" testing group again.

Even if you can fix the bug while introducing no new ones, you are not necessarily doing your users any favors. What you have now, with the bug, might be more useful to them than what you might have in another month after fixing the bug and retesting.

It is critical to look at the program as it is. Then compare it to the program you could have in the future, with all the bugs fixed. When you compare these two programs, it may be obvious which program your users would rather have.

Making a bad choice in either direction can have serious ramifications. If you ship too buggy a product, you get a bad reputation, and your users may switch to a competing product. If you wait, they might give up waiting for you and go to a competitor.

If you are worried that you will lose customers either way, fix the bugs. If you ship late, you may lose customers, but you earn a reputation for solid software. The good reputation will usually gain you more new customers in the end.

This particular decision is one of the most difficult in the development and testing process. The testing group needs to be involved at this point, because often only they and the developers have a clear idea of the bug and its ramifications.

You obviously need to fix some bugs. However, mandatory fixes rarely come to light at this late release-candidate stage. Bugs such as misspellings obviously do not need to be fixed. Sometimes, while no single bug is critical enough to merit fixing, all of them taken together are.

Keep in mind that no matter how well you test, you will ship a product with bugs that you haven't discovered. And no matter how extensive the beta testing, you might discover a serious bug after shipping. Do not keep fixing the product to remove the final little bugs so you can ship a bug-free product. That goal will merely prolong the test period and deliver software that is no better.

At the same time, don't use the excuse that "all software is buggy" to ship a product with unacceptable bugs in it. Today's users do not expect to find bugs in their programs. At least 90 percent of your users should never notice a bug in your product.

A final note: Be sure to test not only the builds leading up to the release candidate, but also the release candidate itself. All of your efforts have been leading toward testing this one specific build.

Management

It is important that the testers do not report to a development leader. The testers should report to the person in charge of the technical support group, because if the testers miss a bug, technical support pays the price. Technical support is the department that will get all the calls from unhappy users who discover all the MFUs you hid in the program for them to find.

If the testers do report to the development leader, then, consciously or subconsciously, they will end up being encouraged to not find bugs—the death of effective testing. Development is not happy when bugs are found. Development wants to finish development, and bug discovery prolongs the process.

At a minimum, the testers' leader should report to the same person the developers' leader reports to: the person responsible for shipping a successful product.

If the testers are not part of the technical support group, they should talk to that group often. Technical support needs to work closely with the testers to minimize problems in the program. Many times, technical support can find places where small, easy changes in the program can significantly reduce the number of technical support requests.

Putting It All Together

Everything I've said in this chapter leads back to where I started: the goal of testing is to identify bugs in the program. You might not fix them all (in some cases, it would be impossible to do so), but you know what kind they all are.

This allows the members of the project to make intelligent decisions about what to fix and what to leave. More important, it allows project management to make an informed decision on when to ship the new product. Without proper testing, management bases its shipping decision on guesswork—and then waits for the inevitable bug reports to come in.

PC software development has improved greatly over the past several years. Users don't expect to find bugs in operating systems. In DOS 5 and Windows 3.1, users see few, if any, bugs.

Popular software applications are also reaching this point. Lotus recently shipped a 1-2-3 spreadsheet program for Windows and had to recall it due to a level of bugs that would have been acceptable two years ago. A year from now, users will expect all of their general applications to be at this same level of robustness. Soon or sooner (not later), users will see bug-free replacements for the applications they currently use. And they will buy them.

Once users' general applications are, in their view, bug-free, they will demand that their specific applications be free of bugs as well. Developers who write vertical-market or in-house applications have only a year or two to develop good, bug-free specific applications. Users aren't stupid. If your word processor is well-designed, full-featured, and bug-free, and your vertical-market application isn't, it will be painfully obvious that it is not as good as it could be.

Two years from now, the successful software companies will have good test procedures in place, and they will use them. What they do will follow much, if not most, of what has been laid out here—not necessarily because all the staff reads this book, but because they follow the ideas detailed here.

Dire Warning!

Many companies already follow the procedures I've described in this book. Over the next year, many more will begin to do so. If you wait a year or two to start, you will have to wait another year to get the procedures working and turn out a properly tested product.

If you want to be in business two years from now, set up testing procedures *now*. Remember, if you don't turn out a successful product, it's not just you who might lose a job, it's everyone else in your company or division, too. This is serious business.

- Implement proper testing procedures—don't simply go through the motions.
- Make use of the test results—don't ignore them.

Chapter 14

Useful Bug-Discovery Tools

Now that the rest of the book has you convinced that you should discover the bugs in your code, we'll discuss a number of tools available in the PC market to help you do it.

Unfortunately, there are not many good ones. Three, however, are worth their weight in gold: Bounds Checker is a must for testing DOS programs; Microsoft Test is a must for testing Windows programs; and MemCheck is invaluable under both systems.

Aside from these, there are a few other useful tools (listed below) as well as the ever-critical debuggers. There is a real need for additional tools to help discover bugs. I hope that over the next several years more tools will become available to help make discovering bugs easier.

Bounds Checker

Every once in a while, someone comes out with a new class of program: VisiCalc with the first spreadsheet; Norton with the first Unerase; and now Nu-Mega with the first bounds checker. Any developer who does not use Bounds Checker to test programs is spending a lot of unnecessary time tracking down a certain class of bugs.

Bounds Checker is actually very simple. It uses the memory mapping and page faults of the 386 to set bounds on a program. It marks your code area as read-only, your data area as read-write, and all other memory off limits. If your program writes to anywhere except your data area or reads from any area other than your code or data area, a page fault occurs, and Bounds Checker shows you which instruction accessed what out-of-bounds memory.

Bounds Checker turns itself off when a program issues an interrupt. The code for the interrupt is usually not part of the program, and Bounds Checker therefore legitimately accesses memory outside of the program's area. It is even smart enough to track any DOS allocs and frees you may do, and lets you access only memory that you presently have malloc'ed.

You can list areas that are okay for your program to access, such as the BIOS data area, video memory, and EMS. If you simply specify EMS rather than a specific memory range, Bounds Checker will even determine the location of the EMS page frame automatically. Exception areas can be of any size (for the BIOS data area, I list just the bytes I read) and can be listed as read-only, read-write, or write-only. And you can allow any part of your program to access these ranges, or just specific modules.

When it finds a fault, Bounds Checker tells you what part of your code made the violation and what memory you were accessing. It also lists the call stack. The call stack is valuable because if memcpy is causing the violation, the call stack shows you what routine called memcpy with the bad pointer. These violations are then written to a log file when the program exits, which lets testers use Bounds Checker without having to understand it.

Bounds Checker does have some limits. It is designed mainly for foreground applications written in a high-level language such as C. It allows one code area followed by one data area (each area can be > 64K). This is the most serious limit. TSRs need this more than foreground applications. Ideally, Nu-Mega will come up with a method for working with TSRs that allows interspersed code and data areas.

Bounds Checker also needs to be more discriminating about segments. The data area should mark the constant data as read-only. The EMS memory should only be accessible if pages belonging to the application are mapped in.

All of this, however, would simply be frosting on the cake: Nu-Mega would only be making an already invaluable product even more essential. Further, Nu-Mega is already working on a number of improvements. As it stands, Bounds Checker is almost certain to find all of your loose pointers—and definitely the far ones.

A program I wrote several years ago occasionally locked up when executing a certain function. It happened very rarely and never to me—I wasn't even sure it was a bug, because it was so rare and I never saw it. Bounds Checker found the memory violation the first time I ran that function. I was writing to the DOS area, in a place that usually wasn't catastrophic. In less than five minutes, I eliminated the bug.

Bounds Checker makes it fast and easy to find bugs of this type and, in terms of time saved, is one of the most cost-effective development tools around. More important, it almost completely eliminates a class of bugs (loose pointers) from programs tested under it.

I believe that it may soon be considered as unacceptable to sell a DOS program that has not been tested with Bounds Checker as it is to sell a program that has not gone through a decent test cycle. Figure 14-1 shows an example of Bounds Checker.

Figure 14-1: Bounds Ckecker

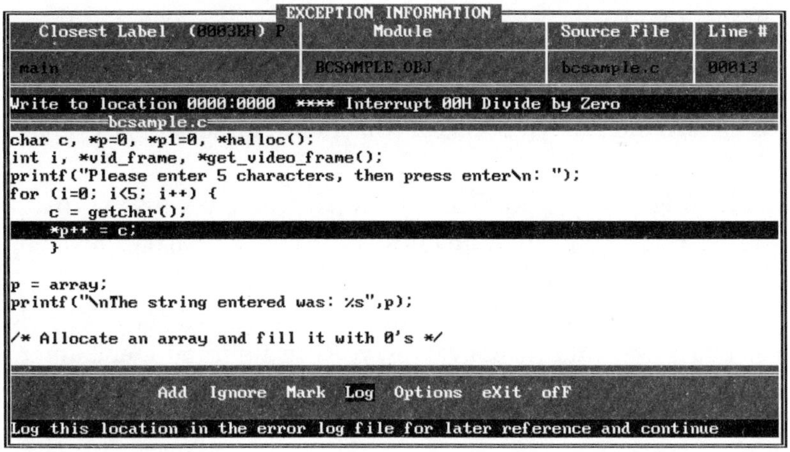

Microsoft Test

In the chapter on testing, I stressed that it is critical to automate your tests. However, this can be a lot of work, especially for a Windows application ("Are you sure that pixel shouldn't be one to the right?").

Until now, most companies either didn't automate—they used batch files—or they wrote their own test programs. Microsoft Test does all of this for you.

Microsoft Test is unique and invaluable. With it you can create the full-featured automated tests that are essential to a good testing process. By setting up test scripts, you can, with no human intervention, run scripts that perform every test you have created against each new version of a program.

Testing a program no longer requires a major investment in time or fallible human beings to watch each step of the program and verify that it is working properly. And tests don't need to be skipped because of inadequate staff or time. Microsoft Test includes everything you need to create and run automated test scripts, including keyboard and mouse input, and checking the screen output. It runs these tests automatically and logs the results.

Keyboard and mouse input are handled by placing the key and mouse events in the message queue of the application being tested. The application sees no difference between Microsoft Test and a user pressing some keys.

For screen dump comparisons, you can have separate screen dumps for each monitor type (EGA, VGA, and so on). You can also use fuzzy logic where it will look for a button in a given area. Because a button might have a slightly different shape on different monitor types, the fuzzy logic lets you use one screen dump.

Microsoft Test can also check dialog boxes by the contents of controls, DDE and OLE messages, and so on. This allows you to test against actual results instead of the screen display (that is, the text contents of an edit control rather than the image of the text on the screen).

It is more valuable to test what values are in a dialog box, because normally you will be using those values. Your program doesn't read the bitmap of the dialog box, it reads the text in an edit control.

The same holds for DDE and OLE: the contents of these messages is critical to using them properly. By checking the actual values, you can assure proper communication with other programs. Without this feature, you would be left waiting to see the effects of bad data passed.

Microsoft Test includes a Basic command language so that you can develop sophisticated test scripts. The Basic environment includes a recorder and debugger so you can debug your debugging scripts.

I had never planned on learning COBOL or Basic. Unfortunately, with the advent of Microsoft Test (and Visual Basic), it is now critical to learn Basic to be able to program Test. For those of you who already know Basic, all you have to learn is a few additional commands. The rest of you, like me, will have to learn the whole language.

I wish there were a test program for DOS applications. You can test your DOS application in a window and use Microsoft Test on it, but for most cases, I think you may still be better off writing your own test software than using Microsoft Test for a DOS application. Microsoft Test is shown in Figure 14-2.

Figure 14-2: Microsoft Test

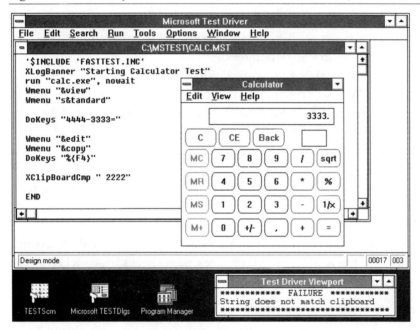

Microsoft test can make life a lot easier for you when you write a Windows application, even if you have some automated tools. Test definitely makes it easier to test your products adequately. With the advent of Test, there is no excuse for not having a full set of automated tests for every product you have under development, nor any excuse to ship a Windows application that has not been fully tested.

And how did Microsoft test Test? They had Test test Test by testing a program. And what was one of the programs they tested Test testing? Why, Test of course. So you had Test testing Test testing Test. Now that's testing recursion.

MemCheck

In an earlier chapter, I discussed an assertion function for strings. Among other things, the assertion macro could, if the passed-in pointer was dynamically malloc'ed, verify that enough memory was available.

Dynamic memory overwrites are one of the most common and difficult-to-find bugs that occur in C. It becomes especially so with strings where the length of the string (via strlen) is one byte less than what's needed for storage.

MemCheck finds these bugs through a number of simple mechanisms. It does this with almost no effect on your existing code. You include memcheck.h in your source files and add two calls. That's it.

Although MemCheck can turn its checking on and off for debug and non-debug mode, you can also put the include and two function calls inside **#if DEBUG** statements, and it then disappears in non-debug mode.

MemCheck provides two basic functions. First, it implements the functionality described in Chapter 8, *Watching the Heap*. All allocations have check bytes placed before and after them. All allocations know the file and line of source they were malloc'ed in. With this capability, MemCheck will tell you whether you underwrite or overwrite the memory you have malloc'ed. It also can list for you, on exit, any unfreed memory, which prevents you from not freeing all your memory.

Second, MemCheck includes its own library of all the basic string and memory calls. You then call MemCheck's strlen and memcpy instead of the one in your compiler's run-time library.

Any time one of these functions receives a pointer, the function will determine whether the pointer is in the heap. If so, MemCheck then checks to see whether the pointer points to enough memory for the function. If you dynamically allocate a pointer to 26 bytes and then try to strcpy 27 bytes to it, MemCheck will find the error.

Unfortunately, MemCheck works only on dynamically malloc'ed pointers. There is a call, **mc_register**, that you can use to list the base and extent of your global and local variables. (You can also unregister, which is crucial for local variables.) However, this requires a function call for each variable. It's too bad that MemCheck can't read the code view information in an .exe file, which lists all variables, including their base and extent.

MemCheck can also check for writing to NULL, and it can check the entire heap at any time. Both of these are good additions to the TestAll function.

It also allows you to provide a function to replace printf, which MemCheck uses to display errors. If you use a windowing system for your program, you can have error messages either pop up in a Message Box or be written to the debug monitor.

MemCheck gives you a lot of checking for very little time or pain. If you don't already have code to perform this parameter validation, use MemCheck. I only wish it did more. Checking just malloc'ed pointers is better than checking no pointers, though. See Figure 14-3 for an example of MemCheck.

Figure 14-3: MemCheck

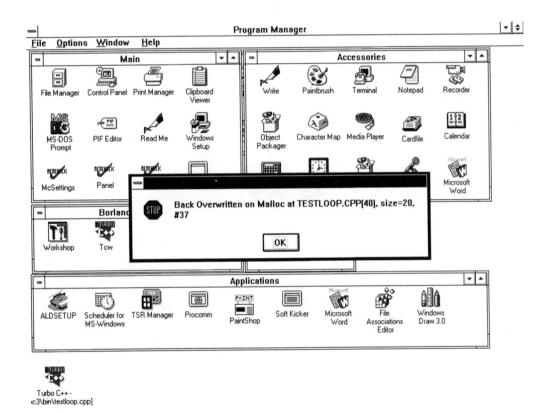

This is the epitome of a good *No Bugs* tool: you can forget it's there until it finds a bug.

Multiscope Post-Mortem Debugger

Although the Post-Mortem Debugger is only a part of the Multiscope Debugger (discussed later), it deserves separate mention. The Post-Mortem Debugger records the state of your system when your application crashes. You can then go into this recorded file with the Crash Analyzer to determine what went wrong as shown in Figure 14-4. When you are trying to figure out why the program crashed, especially if it happened only at a beta site, this dump file can prove invaluable.

Figure 14-4: Multiscope Post-Mortem Debugger

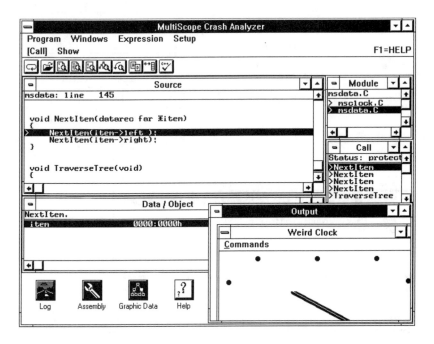

What makes this feature worth separate mention is that you can ship the recorder (MED) with your program to beta sites. Then, when a beta site does something that causes the application to crash, MED records the information for transmission back to you. At a minimum, you should license a few copies of the Post-Mortem Debugger so you can send it out to sites that report errors you are unable to duplicate. You might even want to make it an integral part of your beta kit. This can eliminate hours of phone calls to beta sites to try to figure out what they are doing to cause a crash.

Windows Dr. Watson

The program drwatson.exe, which is included with each copy of Windows, also deserves separate mention. Those of you who took part in the Windows 3.1 beta test have almost certainly seen Dr. Watson in action. When Windows gets a GP fault or protection violation, Dr. Watson prompts the user for a short statement as to what went wrong.

Dr. Watson then writes a log file with all pertinent information about the system, including the instruction in the application that caused the error. In many cases, this log will point you directly to the bug.

If a user reports a bug in one of your programs that causes Windows 3.1 to close the program, have them repeat the error with drwatson.exe running, and have them ship you the error log. Nine times out of ten, that will be sufficient to solve the problem.

Windows Debug Version

The Windows Software Development Kit includes a debug version of Windows. In Windows 3.0, this made a big difference, because the debug version performed parameter checking, while the retail version didn't.

The debug version still performs additional checking that the retail version does not. A Windows application should run, without even a warning, on the debug version of Windows. While testing a Windows application, use the debug version of Windows and have a serial terminal connected to your serial port (which the debug kernel will write to).

The debug version also has several flags that you can turn on to perform additional checking. The first flag is ilovebear, which will cause passed-in strings to be filled to their passed-in limits before having return values placed in them. This guarantees that all passed-in buffers are long enough.

The debug version also has the call ValidateFreeSpaces, which, in conjunction with the flags EnableFreeChecking and EnableHeapChecking, performs additional checking of the heap. This call adds about a 20 percent overhead to Windows. However, it will catch writes to freed memory.

The call ValidateCodeSegments is useful only in real mode. If your program will run in real mode, you should use this test. However, if your program will only run in protected mode, there is no reason to use this call.

Windows also provides the Stress Applicator and Heap Walker, which can be used to eat up resources. The Stress Applicator can use up the heap, leaving a set amount of free memory. It can do this to the global heap, a program's local heap, and the GDI heap (more commonly known as system resources). It can also use up disk space and file handles, once again leaving limited, or no, resources.

The Heap Walker can also use up the global heap and dump discardable segments. Both the Stress Applicator and Heap Walker allow you to test your application under situations where resources have completely run out. While your program will not be expected to be able to continue in these cases, it should at least gracefully decline to perform a function.

Again, these valuable tools allow you to see what your program will do under severe constraints. Between these tools and the debug kernel, you can do an acceptable job of testing your Windows application. Not using these tools to test your Windows application is inviting trouble.

RT-Link

RT-Link deserves mention here. RT-Link is a sophisticated linker for DOS programs and, on the face of it, does not belong in this section. However, RT-Link includes several tools that show how powerful some error checking can be when it's implemented properly.

RT-Link allows you to link your programs to use virtual memory on an 8088. Code (and data, too, in some cases) is kept on disk and paged into memory as needed. Unlike an overlay linker, RT-Link keeps a list of pages and loads the code into the LRU page.

Needless to say, the program is loaded differently each time you run it. Because code that has called other code can be unloaded (and then reloaded on return), you have a very dangerous situation if any one page of code depends on another page being in memory.

This is not a bug in RT-Link. You can tell RT-Link when you believe it's safe for one code page to access another directly, saving the performance hit of going through RT-Link's virtual memory manager.

However, if you are wrong somewhere, you may be accessing a page that is still not in memory. This will create a bug that occurs only on systems with a small amount of memory or on any system when you call a set of functions in a certain order.

RT-Link includes a command (VM_MURPHY) that allocates just one page for all virtual memory swapping. When linked with this command, the program is painfully slow. However, at no time is more than one page in memory. If one page depends on another page being in memory, the program will crash.

This is a commendable example of a tool vendor incorporating technology that helps find bugs. Moreover, this command is a technique that can be incorporated only by the tool vendor. If only more tool vendors would provide features like this . . .

Debuggers

Be sure you have a good debugger. Personally, I'm partial to Soft-Ice for a 386 and Periscope for a 286 or 8086. However, I prefer debugging in assembly language. Although both Soft-Ice and Periscope have C source-level debugging, it is generally one step behind that of the compiler vendor's source level displays.

When you really need to get down and dirty with Windows in 386 mode, you have only two choices of debuggers, WDEB386 or Win-Ice (Soft-Ice for Windows). WDEB386 comes with the Windows SDK and is an awesome command-line debugger. Win-Ice, however, is a full-screen debugger and works at a source-code level.

Periscope has a debugger for Windows. However, for debugging on a system level (for example, on VxDs), it is much more limited than Win-Ice or WDEB386. For application-level debugging, it is not as good as Multiscope. Also, it requires two 80386 systems connected via a serial line.

The valuable thing about debugging in assembly language is that you see what you are actually getting for final code. This not only lets you see whether the compiler is generating bad code (which occasionally happens), but also lets you see how efficient the code is. This will become more important with the advent of C++, where a plus (+) can become a horribly slow and complex set of instructions.

The source-level debuggers shipped with compilers, such as those from Microsoft and Borland, are all good and getting better. Multiscope's source-level debugging is flat-out incredible. Just be sure the debugger does what you want, and you know how to use it.

Finally, if you really need to get down to the hardware and you find that Soft-Ice is interfering with some subtle timing problems, you need a hardware ICE. In this case, there is only one choice: Periscope IV. Some of the Periscope debuggers are hardware based, so they do not affect the system at all. (Soft-Ice does affect it somewhat.) And they cost a lot less than the ICEs from Intel.

If you get down to the system level, you need Soft-Ice (or Win-Ice) on a 386 and Periscope on a 286 (or earlier) machine. If you program at the application level, you can use one of these debuggers, the debugger that comes with your compiler, or Multiscope.

If you find yourself at both the system and application levels, you need two or three debuggers. Just as a carpenter usually owns several saws, developers often need several debuggers.

Periscope

Quite simply, the best assembler-level debugger for an 80286 or earlier system is Periscope. Not only is it a very good debugger, but it is also the only program I have ever used in which I have not found a single bug (and the developer did it without reading this book!).

Periscope has just about every feature you could ever need, including source-level symbolic debugging. One version, the Model II, includes a switch you can use to break into the debugger at any time—even if interrupts are off.

Another version, the Model I, uses an inexpensive board with write-protected memory. The debugger is loaded into the board's memory, leaving all lower memory free. Although a program can usually spare the lower memory, some bugs disappear when the program is loaded higher.

If a bug tries to write over the write-protected memory, the memory won't get hurt. You can still bring the debugger up, regardless of the damage your bug has caused. This sounds like a great feature, but I have found that by the time a bug has trashed everything else, there is no information left that can help discover what caused the problem in the first place.

Periscope also has Model IV, shown in Figure 14-5, which includes cards that go in the PC and give you most of the features of an ICE for a lot less money. If you find yourself needing an ICE for a 286 or 386, again, Periscope is the place to go.

Although the Periscope ICE does not have every feature of the Intel ICE, it provides most of the same functionality at a much lower price. Although Soft-Ice changes the system slightly, the Periscope-assisted cards have no effect at all. That makes a sometimes-critical difference.

Because the Periscope IV card sits on the bus, it can watch the actual bus signals without any change in system performance. This can be tremendously valuable in some cases, because you receive more information—more than just which instruction executed. If Soft-Ice isn't powerful enough to find a bug, a Periscope IV card is.

Figure 14-5: Periscope IV

```
 File   Breakpoints   Symbols   Windows   Memory  Reg/misc   Options   Hardware
3A0E:0100   EB 36 54 6F 74 61 6C 20-6D 65 6D 6F
3A0E:0110   30 30 30 20 4B 42 20 20-20 20 4D 65    Go with hardware enabled (GH)
D0 — SAMPLE                                        Display hw breakpoints (HA)
7(A) D000:05C0            PERISCOPE   5.20K         Clear all breakpoints (HA *)
                                                   Disable all breakpoints (HA -)
                                                   Enable all breakpoints (HA +)
                                                   Bit breakpoints (HB)
W — WR SS:FFFC = D000                               Controls [HC]
   #29: start:   call getmem               ; get   Data breakpoints (HD)
                                                   Memory breakpoints (HM)
   #31:          mov ax,totmem             ; tota  Port breakpoints (HP)
   #32:          mov di,offset tmemory     ; conv  Read trace buffer [HR-HU]
   #33:          call convert              ; conv ┌Select format──────────────  (HW)
                                                  │ Raw mode (HR)
   #35:          mov ax,fremem             ; free │ Single entry (HS)        │0001
   #36:          mov di,offset amemory     ; conve│ Trace mode (HT)          │0402
   #37:          call convert              ; conve│ Unasm mode (HU)          │FFFF
                                                  │ Display full trace (HT !)│FFFF
U↑═ In C:\PERI\RUN.COM (SAMPLE) ══════════        └──────────────────────────  FFFF

>t
>
```

Periscope for Windows gives you full debugging of everything except VxDs. It can debug VxDs after the Sys_Critical_Init is over. It provides full-screen, source-level, symbolic debugging. The debugger requires two 80386 systems, one running the debugger and the other running Windows (and a small part of the debugger).

Because it uses two systems, the debugger can read source files, map files, and so on, without affecting the Windows system. Also, the Windows system is minimally affected by the small Periscope stub program running on it.

Soft-Ice

Brought to you by the people who did Bounds Checker, Soft-Ice uses the capabilities of the 386 to give you an 8086 ICE using only software. It comes admirably close to this goal, falling short only on some very subtle timing problems.

If you are debugging real-mode DOS programs, this debugger will be invaluable sooner or later. You can set it to break when a program reads or writes to a memory location, and then have it run at full speed until the read/write does occur. (Try that with a normal debugger.)

Soft-Ice performs this magic by using some of the features in the 80386. First of all, the 80386 has a couple of debug registers that can be used to cause a break when accessing a specific memory location. There are few of these, and they can be set to break only on a byte to dword range.

Soft-Ice also uses the paging capabilities of the 80386. To break on a memory range, Soft-Ice marks the memory page as "not there." Then when the page is accessed, Soft-Ice determines whether the desired range on the page was touched. If so, it stops the operation. If not, it allows the operation, and then continues.

This works unless the break range is on a page where other contents of the page are accessed constantly. Because pages are in 4K chunks, this can be a real problem. The most common performance problem is setting a break on access to a local variable. Because a local variable is on the stack, every stack access will cause a page fault.

So Soft-Ice is not always a perfect debugging solution. However, in most cases, it gives you all of the ICE capabilities you need—for a lot less money than any real ICE. See Figure 14-6 for an example of Soft-Ice.

Soft-Ice also has a version for Windows, called Win-Ice. Win-Ice debugs not only Windows applications but also Windows device drivers, virtual device drivers, and DOS applications running in a Windows DOS box. I think it's incredible in its range of features and capabilities.

Figure 14-6: Soft-Ice

```
0) hwindow           #1EFF:00000362    288C
1) service_ptr       #1EFF:00000112    003B:0380
------API_ADDRESSES------------------------------dword----------PROT----(0)---
1EFF:00000145 0117:022B 0117:0247 0117:0543 0117:055F    +...G....C..._....
------test.c---------------------------------------------------------PROT16-
00318:    TASKENTRY   tentry;
00319:    HTASK htask;
00320:
00321:    BeginPaint (hWnd, (LPPAINTSTRUCT) &ps);
00322:    hDC = ps.hdc;
00323:
00324:    Y = 0;
00325:    for (i=0; i<4; ++i)
00326:      {
00327:    sprintf(szOneLine, "%s  %d    ",APINames[i],api_count[i]);
00328:    TextOut(hDC, 0, Y, (LPSTR) szOneLine, lstrlen(szOneLine));
------------------------------TEST------------------------------
:hwnd test
Window Handle    hQueue   QOwner    Class Name      Window Procedure
0E8C(0)          13C7     TEST      #32769          0487:9E6B
 0F0C(1)         13C7     TEST      #32768          USER!BEAR306
 288C(1)         13C7     TEST      TestWClass      TestWindowProc
:
    Enter A Command Or ? For Help
```

Multiscope

Multiscope, shown in Figure 14-7, is a debugger for DOS, Windows, and OS/2 (whatever that is). In Windows, it runs as a Windows application, which gives you an awesome interface. Although not as good on low-level debugging, it shines at source-level debugging of an application.

Figure 14-7: Multiscope

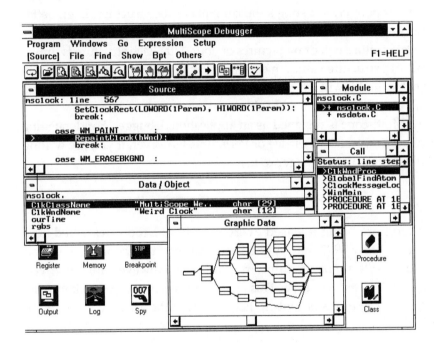

Multiscope is hard to describe in only a few paragraphs. It is, in my view, the best applications debugger on the market. It provides a multitude of interfaces, but the best way to use it is with its Windows interface.

Under Windows, you can debug both DOS (in a DOS box) and Windows programs. You can debug programs running on the same machine or on a different system over a serial line. You can also use dual monitors, but then your second monitor is using a character-based interface instead of Windows.

Part of Multiscope's appeal is that it is Windows-based. Providing the same windowed data via Windows, instead of using a character-based display, makes it a better interface than any other debugger. Also, Windows allows better sizing and layout than you will get on an 80 x 25 monochrome display adapter (MDA).

Also, the Windows interface is generally a lot easier to use than a character-based one. All of the reasons that users prefer Windows-based applications hold for a debugger. In addition, Windows makes it very easy to do things such as modify memory—you click and type.

Multiscope is light-years ahead of all other debuggers for its graphic data display. In addition to giving you the normal ways of viewing your data, when you click on a structure or pointer, it displays the contents of the structure. Even better than that, it has a Graphic Data window.

The Graphic Data feature will draw pictures of your data. Each structure is drawn as a row of boxes, with structure values in each box. Each pointer in the structure will be identified by name, and it will have an arrow pointing to its pointee. Sometimes a picture is worth a a thousand words, and Multiscope proves that.

Unfortunately, Multiscope is designed as an application debugger. For debugging systems-level programs, you need Soft-Ice or Periscope. However, if you are writing applications, Multiscope is the debugger to use.

New Tools

New debugging tools are being released every month. The tools described here are state-of-the-art in early 1992, but by the time you read this book, newer, and possibly better, tools will almost certainly be available. However, for now, you should look at the tools discussed here. This chapter was written so you know the least you should expect in terms of tools to help you find the MFUs you placed in your code.

Remember

Prevention and finding bugs is still a very young practice in the PC world. Developers and testers need to work, along with management, to produce guidelines for product development, keeping in mind what the *end user* wants—a solid product.

Debug Message Boxes

debgmsg.c

```c
#if DEBUG > 0

// These are left public so you can change them with your
// debugger while your program is running. They are kept
// in one structure so there is only 1 global variable that
// you have to worry about naming conflicts with.
DEBUG_VARS sDebug={0,0,-1,true,true,true,true,false};

#if WIN != 0
staticBYTE sTmp[MAX_DEBUG_STR+2]="\0";
#else

// This is used to store resource strings in memory for DOS
// (in Windows you use actual resources). This is covered in
// detail below.
typedef struct S_RES_STRINGS
    {
    unsigned        iResNum;
    BYTE _far       *pResStr;
    } RES_STRINGS;

extern RES_STRINGS _far ResStr[];      // Done so you can put the
```

```
                                  // strings at the end of the file.
#endif

// Same parameters as a printf. Will put up the message and
// wait for a key to be pressed.
void DebugMessageBox (BYTE const *psFrmt, ...)
{
va_list pVa;

  // for case 0 - you can go ahead and print in Window 3.
  // Otherwise if pause is off, you don't do anything. An
  // alternative is to always use vDebugPrint if pause is off
  if ((sDebug.iBox != 0) && (! sDebug.fPause))
    return;

  va_start (pVa, psFrmt);

  // you now need to put up the message. you have the following
  // alternatives:
  // 0 - It goes to Window 3 and then pauses
  // 1 - It pops up on the screen
  // 2 - DOS only - tty output to the screen
  switch (sDebug.iBox)
    {
    case 0 :
      vDebugPrint (3, psFrmt, pVa);
      DebugPause ();
      break;

#if WIN > 0
    case 1 :
      Vsprintf (MAX_DEBUG_STR, sDebug.sMsg, psFrmt, pVa);
      if (MessageBox (0, sDebug.sMsg, "ERROR", MB_TASKMODAL |
                          MB_ICONEXCLAMATION | MB_OKCANCEL) == IDCANCEL)
          sDebug.fPause = false;
      break;
#else

    case 1 :
      PopMessageBox (psFrmt, pVa);
      break;
    case 2 :
```

```
        TtyMessageBox (psFrmt, pVa);
        break;
#endif
    }
}


// The same as DebugMessageBox except it has a resource number
// instead of a dormat string. When debugging, the format
// strings can end up taking enough of the default data segment
// that you run out of space. In Windows, you can store these
// strings as resources. Although you can't do that in DOS, you
// can at least move them to a far data segment so they don't use
// up near data.
void DebugMessageRes (unsigned iNum, ...)
{
va_list pVa;
#if WIN == 0
RES_STRINGS _far *pResOn;
#endif

  // Get the vars
  va_start (pVa, iNum);


// if not windows, you have to get the string from below. The
// strings are all in a far data segment so you have to copy it
// over.
#if WIN == 0

  for (pResOn=ResStr; pResOn->iResNum; pResOn++)
    if (pResOn->iResNum == iNum)
      break;

  if (pResOn->iResNum)
    fStrnCpy (sDebug.sMsg, pResOn->pResStr, MAX_DEBUG_STR);
  else
    {
    StrCpy (sDebug.sMsg, "Unknown resource: %d");
    pVa = (va_list) &iNum;
    }
#endif
```

```
   switch (sDebug.iBox)
     {
     case 0 :
       StrCat (sDebug.sMsg, "\n");
       vDebugPrint (3, sDebug.sMsg, pVa);
       DebugPause ();
       break;

#if WIN > 0
     case 1 :
       if (LoadString (sDebug.hInst, iNum, sTmp,
                          MAX_DEBUG_STR) <= 0)
           Sprintf (MAX_DEBUG_STR, sDebug.sMsg,
                          "DebugPrintRes - No string: %d", iNum);
       else
           Vsprintf (MAX_DEBUG_STR, sDebug.sMsg, sTmp, pVa);

       if (MessageBox (0, sDebug.sMsg, "ERROR", MB_TASKMODAL |
                          MB_ICONEXCLAMATION | MB_OKCANCEL) == IDCANCEL)
           sDebug.fPause = false;
       break;
#else

     case 1 :
       PopMessageBox (sDebug.sMsg, pVa);
       break;
     case 2 :
       TtyMessageBox (sDebug.sMsg, pVa);
       break;
#endif
     }
}


// If you don't have Windows, you have to store your resource
// strings in memory. This is all done right here so if you
// have string resources in DOS, you can pull this out. If not,
// at least it is far data so you don't have to worry about it
// filling up the default data area.
#if WIN == 0
```

```
RES_STRINGS _far ResStr[]={

// buffer\mem
ERR_MEMCPY1,   STR_MEMCPY1,
ERR_MEMCPY2,   STR_MEMCPY2,

...                ...

  0,               NULL};
#endif

#endif
```

_errnum.h

```
#ifndef   I__ERRNUM
#define   I__ERRNUM

#define      ERR_MEMCPY1     16
#define      ERR_MEMCPY2     17

...      ...              ...

#endif
_errstr.h
#ifndef I__ERRSTR
#define I__ERRSTR


#ifndef I__ERRNUM
#include "_errnum.h"
#endif

// buffer\mem
#define    STR_MEMCPY1      "fHbMemCpy (%Fp,%Fp,%u)"
#define    STR_MEMCPY2      "HbMemCpy (%p,%p,%u)"

...   ...      ...

#endif
```

pop_box.c

```
#if DEBUG > 0
#if WIN == 0

#include  "_doslib.h"

void *allocate(unsigned uLen);
void free (void *pBuf);

static void TextCpy (BYTE _far *fpScrn,BYTE const *pBuf,unsigned
iNum);
static int iLevel=0;
static BYTE sPrmt[] = "Press <CR> to continue or ESC to exit";

// The same parameters as printf. Will force the monitor into
// 80x25 mode and pop up a Message Box displaying the passed-in
// text. Press <CR> to continue or ESC to exit to DOS.
// Will save the underlaying screen if allocate can find enough
// memory.
PopMessageBox (BYTE const *pFrmt, void const *pVa)
{
BYTE _far *fpScrn, _far *fpTmp;
BYTE *pBuf, *pRtn, *pUnd;
int iRows, iCols, iNr, iNc, iNum;
BYTE bMode, bPage, bChar;

  // you aren't re-entrant
  if (iLevel)
    return (-1);
  iLevel++;

  // Get the mode and page you are in
  _asm
    {
    mov       ah, 0Fh
    int       10h
    mov       bMode, al
    mov       bPage, bh
    }

  // If you are in mode 3 or 7 - we're done - go for it
```

```
// Otherwise, you need to switch to mode 3
if ((bMode != 3) && (bMode != 7))
  _asm
    {
    mov    ax, 0003h
    int    10h
    mov    ah, 0Fh
    int    10h
    mov    bPage, bh
    }

// If you are not on page 0 - switch it
if (bPage)
  _asm
    {
    mov    ax, 0500h
    int    10h
    }

// OKAY, you now create the message to determine how big a box
// you need to pop up.
Vsprintf (MAX_DEBUG_STR, sDebug.sMsg, pFrmt, pVa);

// you need to determine the maximum width and height
iRows = 2;
iCols = StrLen (sPrmt) + 2;
pBuf = sDebug.sMsg;
while (*pBuf)
  {
  if ((pRtn = StrChr (pBuf, '\n')) == NULL)
    pRtn = pBuf + StrLen (pBuf);
  iCols = Max (iCols, pRtn - pBuf + 4);
  iRows++;
  if (*(pBuf = pRtn) == '\n')
    pBuf++;
  }

// Figure out the pop-up position
iNr = *((BYTE _far *) PTR (0x40, 0x84)) + 1;
iNc = *((unsigned _far *) PTR (0x40, 0x4A));
fpScrn = (bMode == 7) ? PTR (0xB000,0) : PTR (0xB800,0);
fpScrn += (((iNr - iRows) & ~1) * iNc) + ((iNc - iCols) & ~1);
```

```
// you need some memory to store the underlay
// If you don't get it - you pop up anyways - you simply can't
// restore the screen.
if ((pUnd = allocate (iRows * iCols * 2)) != NULL)
  for (iNum=iNr, pRtn=pUnd, fpTmp=fpScrn; iNum--;
                                    pRtn+=iCols*2, fpTmp+=iNc*2)
    fMemCpy (pRtn, fpTmp, iCols*2);

// Put up the border, clear the center & set the attributes
fMemwSet (fpScrn, 0x70CD, iCols);
*fpScrn = 0xC9;
*(fpScrn+(iCols-1)*2) = 0xBB;
for (iNum=iRows-2, fpTmp=fpScrn+iNc*2; iNum--; fpTmp+=iNc*2)
  {
  fMemwSet (fpTmp+2, 0x0720, iCols-2);
  *((unsigned _far *)fpTmp) = 0x70BA;
  *(((unsigned _far *)fpTmp)+iCols-1) = 0x70BA;
  }
fMemwSet (fpTmp, 0x70CD, iCols);
*fpTmp = 0xC8;
*(fpTmp+(iCols-1)*2) = 0xBC;
iNum = StrLen (sPrmt);
TextCpy (fpTmp+((iCols-iNum)&~1), sPrmt, iNum);

// Print out the message
fpTmp = fpScrn + iNc * 2 + 4;
pBuf = sDebug.sMsg;
while (*pBuf)
  {
  if ((pRtn = StrChr (pBuf, '\n')) == NULL)
    pRtn = pBuf + StrLen (pBuf);
  iNum = pRtn - pBuf;
  TextCpy (fpTmp, pBuf, iNum);
  fpTmp += iNc * 2;
  pBuf += iNum;
  if (*pBuf)
    pBuf++;
  }

// you now need to wait for a <CR> or ESC to be pressed
while (true)
```

```c
    {
    _asm
       {
       mov     ah, 0
       int     16h
       mov     bChar, al
       }

    switch (bChar)
       {
       case 0x0D:
            goto Done;
       case 0x1B:
            _asm
               {
               mov        ax, 4CFFh
               int        21h
               }
            goto Done;

       // beep - bad char
       default:
            _asm
               {
               mov        ax, 0E07h
               mov        bx, 0007h
               int        10h
               }
       }
    }

Done:
   // If you have an underlay, you restore it
   if (pUnd)
      {
      for (iNum=iNr, pRtn=pUnd, fpTmp=fpScrn; iNum--;
                                     pRtn+=iCols*2, fpTmp+=iNc*2)
         fMemCpy (fpTmp, pRtn, iCols*2);
      free (pUnd);
      }

   // Restore the mode and page. you only restore it if it's
```

```
      // different Some BIOSs do weird things if you set to the
      // existing mode/page
      _asm
         {
         mov      ah, 0Fh
         int      10h
         cmp      bMode, al
         je    ModeOk
         mov      ah, 00h
         mov      al, bMode
         int      10h
ModeOk:
         mov      ah, 0Fh
         int      10h
         cmp      bPage, bh
         je    PageOk
         mov      ah, 05h
         mov      al, bPage
         int      10h
PageOk:
         }

   iLevel--;
   return (0);
}

static void TextCpy (BYTE _far *fpScrn,BYTE const *pBuf,unsigned
iNum)
{

   while (iNum--)
      {
      *fpScrn = *pBuf++;
      fpScrn += 2;
      }
}

#endif
#endif
```

tty_box.c

```
#if DEBUG > 0
```

```c
#if WIN == 0

#include  "_doslib.h"

static iLevel=0;
static void TtyOut (BYTE const *pBuf);

// The same parameters as printf. Will use the video BIOS to print
// the text out via tty (that is, like a normal printf). Press
// <CR> to continue or ESC to exit to DOS.
TtyMessageBox (BYTE const *pFrmt, void const *pVa)
{
BYTE bChar;

  // you aren't re-entrant
  if (iLevel)
    return (-1);
  iLevel++;

  // you first need to be sure the cursor is on the screen.
  // If it isn't, you put it at 0,0
  // Note: this should work with virtually all cards in most modes.
  //       However, to be system independent, it doesn't work with
  //       cards that don't support the BIOS, like the hercules card
  //       in graphics mode.
  _asm
    {
    mov     ah, 0Fh
    int     10h                 // Get active page
    mov     ah, 03h
    int     10h                 // Get cursor position
    push    es
    mov     ax, 40h
    mov     es, ax
    cmp     dl, es:[4Ah]        // ?? past end of line
    jb      ColOk               // NO - col ok
    inc     dh
    xor     dl, dl              // set to start of next line
ColOk:
    cmp     dh, es:[84h]        // ?? past last row
    jbe     RowOk               // NO - row ok
    xor     dx, dx              // set to 0, 0
```

```
RowOk:
    pop     es
    mov     ah, 02h         // set cursor position
    int     10h             // do this regardless in case the
    }                       // BIOS didn't know (like Lotus 123)

    // OKAY, you have the cursor in the right place. you now do a
    // sprintf to a buffer and print using int 10h. you do this
    // instead of a printf because you want to disturb the system as
    // little as possible AND things might be really fouled up, to
    // the point that DOS can write to the screen.

    // This method has two dangers, first you are not re-entrant and
    // second, you have a limit to how long a message can be.

    Vsprintf (MAX_DEBUG_STR, sDebug.sMsg, pFrmt, pVa);

    // Print it out via TTY
    TtyOut (sDebug.sMsg);
    TtyOut ("\nPress <CR> to continue or ESC to exit");

    // you now need to wait for a <CR> or ESC to be pressed
    while (true)
      {
      _asm
        {
        mov     ah, 0
        int     16h
        mov     bChar, al
        }

      switch (bChar)
        {
        case 0x0D:
            TtyOut ("\n");
            iLevel--;
            return (0);
        case 0x1B:
            iLevel--;
            _asm
              {
              mov           ax, 4CFFh
              int           21h
              }
            return (-1);            // In case the exit fails
```

```
        }                              // This will only happen if you
                                       // are doing something really weird
    // beep - bad char
    TtyOut ("\007");
        }
}
// Print it out via TTY
static void TtyOut (BYTE const *pBuf)
{
BYTE bPage, bChar;

    _asm
      {
      mov       ah, 0Fh
      int       10h                    // Get active page
      mov       bPage, bh
      }
    while (*pBuf)
      {
      if ((bChar = *pBuf++) == '\n')
        _asm
            {
            mov       ax, 0E0Dh
            mov       bh, bPage
            mov       bl, 07h
            int       10h
            }
      _asm
        {
        mov       ah, 0Eh
        mov       al, bChar
        mov       bh, bPage
        mov       bl, 07h
        int       10h
        }
      }
}
#endif
#endif
```

Debug Second Monitor

debgprnt.c

```
#if DEBUG > 0

// Defined here and in mda.c
#define     PRINT_SCREEN        0x01
#define     FILE_OFF            0x02
#define     PAUSE_OFF           0x04
#define     ERROR_OFF           0x08
#define     PAUSED              0x10


int    MdaNumRows (void);
int    MdaNumCols (void);
FLAG   MdaInit(void);
void   MdaBeep(void);
void   MdaFill(int  iRow,int  iCol,unsigned short  uChrAtr,int
iNum);
void   MdaWrite(int  iRow,int  iCol,BYTE const  _far *pBuf,int
iNum);
void   MdaScroll(int  iRow,int  iCol,int  iNr,int  iNc);
unsigned short  MdaGetChar(int  iRow,int  iCol);
BYTE   MdaKey(void);
FLAG   MdaPrnt(BYTE  bChr,FLAG fTran);
```

```
static void  DebugOut (BYTE const _far *psBuf,int iLen,int _far
*piWin);
static void  DoMsg (int iRow,int iCol,int iNr,int iNc,int
*piCurRow, int *piCurCol,BYTE const _far *psBuf,int iLen);
static void  fScroll (void);
static void  _PrintScreen (void);
static BYTE  _PrintChar (BYTE bChr);


static int iLevel=0, iLastFileWin=-1;


#define     NUM_WINDOWS     5
#define     MSG_ROW         20
#define     MSG_COL         65

static int iRect[NUM_WINDOWS][6] = {  0,  0, 11, 49,  0,  0,
                                     12,  0, 20, 49, 12,  0,
                                     21,  0, 25, 25, 21,  0,
                                     21, 26, 25, 80, 21, 26,
                                      0, 50, 20, 80,  0, 50};

// Clear screen, set up borders
void DebugVideoInit ()
{
int iNum, iRow, iStrt, iLast;

  // See whether you have a MDA
  if (MdaInit ())
    {
    if (sDebug.iBox == 0)
      sDebug.iBox = 1;
    sDebug.fDebug = sDebug.fMda = false;
    return;
    }
  sDebug.fMda = true;

  // Clear it
  MdaFill (0, 0, 0x0720, MdaNumRows () * MdaNumCols ());

  // Set up dividers
```

```
for (iNum=0; iNum<NUM_WINDOWS; iNum++)
  if (iRect[iNum][0] > 0)
    MdaFill (iRect[iNum][0]-1, iRect[iNum][1], 0x70CD,
                              iRect[iNum][3] - iRect[iNum][1]);

// Put up the vertical lines and joints
for (iNum=0; iNum<NUM_WINDOWS; iNum++)
  if (iRect[iNum][1] > 0)
    {
    iStrt = iRect[iNum][0]>0 ? iRect[iNum][0]-1 : iRect[iNum][0];
    iLast = iRect[iNum][2]>=MdaNumRows () ? iRect[iNum][2]-1 :
               iRect[iNum][2];
    for (iRow=iStrt; iRow<=iLast; iRow++)
        {
        switch ((MdaGetChar (iRow, iRect[iNum][1]-2) << 8) |
                   (MdaGetChar (iRow, iRect[iNum][1]) & 0xFF))
          {
          case 0xCD20 :
            MdaFill (iRow, iRect[iNum][1]-1, 0x70B9, 1);
            break;
          case 0x20CD :
            MdaFill (iRow, iRect[iNum][1]-1, 0x70CC, 1);
            break;
          case 0xCDCD :
            if (iRow == iStrt)
                {
                if ((iRow > 0) && ((MdaGetChar (iRow-1,iRect[iNum]
                                   [1]-1) & 0xFF00) == 0xBA))
                    MdaFill (iRow, iRect[iNum][1]-1, 0x70CE, 1);
                else
                    MdaFill (iRow, iRect[iNum][1]-1, 0x70CB, 1);
                }
            else
                if (iRow == iLast)
                    MdaFill (iRow, iRect[iNum][1]-1, 0x70CA, 1);
                else
                    MdaFill (iRow, iRect[iNum][1]-1, 0x70CE, 1);
            break;
          default :
            MdaFill (iRow, iRect[iNum][1]-1, 0x70BA, 1);
            break;
          }
```

```
            }
        }
}

// When called, will wait for pause (Scroll Lock) to be turned on
// and then off again.
FLAG DebugPause (void)
{
FLAG fRtn=false;

    if ((! sDebug.fPause) || (! sDebug.fMda))
      return (false);

    MdaWrite (MSG_ROW, MSG_COL, " Paused ", 8);
    MdaBeep ();

    while (! (MdaKey () & PAUSED))
      {
      if (MdaKey () & FILE_OFF)
        {
        sDebug.fWrite = false;
        MdaWrite (MSG_ROW, MSG_COL, " Write OFF ", 11);
        }
      if (MdaKey () & ERROR_OFF)
        {
        sDebug.fError = false;
        MdaWrite (MSG_ROW, MSG_COL, " Error OFF ", 11);
        }
      if (MdaKey () & PRINT_SCREEN)
        _PrintScreen ();
      if (MdaKey () & PAUSE_OFF)
        {
        sDebug.fPause = false;
        MdaWrite (MSG_ROW, MSG_COL, " Pause OFF ", 11);
        break;
        }
      }

    fScroll ();

    return (fRtn);
}
```

```
// Does a printf to window iWin on the MDA. After iWin, the
// parameters are the same as printf.
void DebugPrint (int iWin,BYTE const *psFrmt, ...)
{
va_list pVa;

  if (iLevel)
    return;

  va_start (pVa, psFrmt);

  vDebugPrint (iWin, psFrmt, pVa);
}

// A vprintf to the MDA.
// you are definitely NOT re-entrant so you use iLevel to be sure
// that you aren't called while handling this (such as
// vDebugPrintf calling a function with a bad parameter).
void vDebugPrint (int iWin,BYTE const *psFrmt,void const *pVa)
{
BYTE sBuf[8];

  // If no MDA - leave
  if (! sDebug.fMda)
    return;

  // If debug printfs are turned off and it's not an error - leave
  if (! sDebug.fDebug)
    {
    if ((iWin != 3) || (! sDebug.fError))
      return;
    }

  // If you are being re-entered - hit the debugger, then return.
  if (iLevel)
    {
    _asm { int 3 };
    return;
    }

  // If a bad window number - put up a message.
```

```
if ((iWin < 0) || (iWin > NUM_WINDOWS-1))
  {
  DebugPrint (3, "\\*Bad DebugPrint Window Number: %d \\*\n", iWin);
  MdaBeep ();
  return;
  }
iLevel++;

// write to the error file
if ((sDebug.hFile >= 0) && (sDebug.fWrite))
  {
  // End the prev line with a \n if you are changing windows and the
  // previous line didn't end with a \n
  if ((iLastFileWin != -1) && (iLastFileWin != iWin))
    {
    iLastFileWin = iWin;
    FileWrite (sDebug.hFile, "\n", 1);
    }
  Sprintf (6, sBuf, "%d: ", iWin);
  FileWrite (sDebug.hFile, sBuf, StrLen (sBuf));
  }

// Print it
_Printf (DebugOut, psFrmt, 0x7FF0, &iWin, pVa);

// you do a commit here so if you lock up after returning this
// message made it to disk. Slow but critical. you do not
// open with commit set because you only need to commit after
// the _Printf - which will call FileWrite below approximately
// twice for each % in psFrmt
if ((sDebug.hFile >= 0) && (sDebug.fWrite))
  {
  if (iLastFileWin != -1)
    iLastFileWin = iWin;
  FileCommit (sDebug.hFile, false);
  }

iLevel--;
}


// This function is called by _Printf to print. It then calls
// DoMsg with the correct parameters for iWin.
```

```
static void DebugOut (LPCBYTE psBuf,int iLen,int far *piWin)
{

   /* write to the mono monitor */
   DoMsg (iRect[*piWin][0], iRect[*piWin][1], iRect[*piWin][2],
            iRect[*piWin][3], &iRect[*piWin][4], &iRect[*piWin][5],
            psBuf, iLen);
}

// Prints the text in the proper window. Handles scrolling within
// a window. Looks for the shift keys.
static void DoMsg (int iRow,int iCol,int iNr,int iNc,int
*piCurRow, int *piCurCol,BYTE const far *psBuf,int iLen)
{
int iNum;
BYTE _far *fpCr;


   // write to the error file. In the interests of speed, you do
   // not convert \n to \r\n. Most text editors can handle \n by
   // itself.
   if ((sDebug.hFile >= 0) && (sDebug.fWrite))
     {
     if (*(psBuf+iLen-1) == '\n')
       iLastFileWin = -1;
     else
       iLastFileWin = -2;
     fFileWrite (sDebug.hFile, psBuf, iLen);
     }

   /* write to the mono monitor */
   while (iLen > 0)
     {
     // Check shift keys
     fScroll ();

     // see whether need to scroll. you do it like this so a new blank
     // line does not appear on the screen, scrolling the top,
     // non-blank line off. you scroll to a new line when you have
     // something to write to it.
     if (*piCurRow >= iNr)
       {
```

```
      MdaScroll (iRow, iCol, iNr-iRow, iNc-iCol);
      *piCurRow = iNr - 1;
      *piCurCol = iCol;
      }

  // do next
  if (*psBuf == '\n')
    {
    (*piCurRow)++;
    *piCurCol = iCol;
    psBuf++;
    iLen--;
    }

  else
    {
    // you can only write a line at a time.
    if ((fpCr = fStrChr (psBuf, '\n')) != NULL)
        iNum = Min (iLen, fpCr - psBuf);
    else
        iNum = iLen;
    iNum = Min (iNum, iNc - *piCurCol);

    // Write it
    MdaWrite (*piCurRow, *piCurCol, psBuf, iNum);
    psBuf += iNum;
    *piCurCol += iNum;
    iLen -= iNum;

    // Did you need to wrap to the next line?
    if ((*piCurCol >= iNc) && (*(psBuf + 1) != '\n'))
        {
        /* wait on scroll lock */
        fScroll ();

        (*piCurRow)++;
        *piCurCol = iCol;
        }
    }
  }

// Check the shift keys again before leaving.
```

```
    fScroll ();
}

// This is where you check and act on the shift keys.
static void fScroll (void)
{

    if (! (MdaKey () & PAUSED))
        return;

    MdaFill (MSG_ROW, MSG_COL, 0x70CD, 11);
    MdaWrite (MSG_ROW, MSG_COL, " Paused ", 8);

    while (MdaKey () & PAUSED)
        {
        if (MdaKey () & PAUSE_OFF)
            sDebug.fPause = false;
        if (MdaKey () & FILE_OFF)
            {
            sDebug.fWrite = false;
            MdaWrite (MSG_ROW, MSG_COL, " Write OFF ", 11);
            }
        if (MdaKey () & ERROR_OFF)
            {
            sDebug.fError = false;
            MdaWrite (MSG_ROW, MSG_COL, " Error OFF ", 11);
            }
        if (MdaKey () & PRINT_SCREEN)
            _PrintScreen ();
        }

    if (! sDebug.fPause)
        MdaWrite (MSG_ROW, MSG_COL, " Pause OFF ", 11);
    else
        MdaFill (MSG_ROW, MSG_COL, 0x70CD, 8);
}

// Prints the MDA display on the printer.
static void _PrintScreen (void)
{
int iRow, iCol;
```

```
  // Put a print message on the debug monitor
  MdaWrite (MSG_ROW, MSG_COL, " Printing ", 10);

  // Start fresh
  if (MdaPrnt ('\r', false))
    goto dne;
  if (MdaPrnt ('\n', false))
    goto dne;
  if (MdaPrnt ('\r', false))
    goto dne;
  if (MdaPrnt ('\n', false))
    goto dne;

  for (iRow=0; iRow<MdaNumRows (); iRow++)
    {
    for (iCol=0; iCol<MdaNumCols (); iCol++)
      if (MdaPrnt ((BYTE) MdaGetChar (iRow, iCol), true))
          goto dne;

    if (MdaPrnt ('\r', false))
      goto dne;
    if (MdaPrnt ('\n', false))
      goto dne;
    }

  // Space from what will follow (possibly another screen dump)
  if (MdaPrnt ('\r', false))
    goto dne;
  if (MdaPrnt ('\n', false))
    goto dne;

  // Clear the print message from the debug monitor
  MdaFill (MSG_ROW, MSG_COL+8, 0x70CD, 2);
  MdaWrite (MSG_ROW, MSG_COL, " Paused ", 8);
  return;

dne:
  MdaFill (MSG_ROW, MSG_COL+7, 0x70CD, 3);
  MdaWrite (MSG_ROW, MSG_COL, " Error ", 7);
  MdaBeep ();
}
```

```
// These are Windows' only resources prints.
#if WIN > 0

void DebugPrintRes (int iWin,int iFrmt, ...)
{
va_list pVa;

  if (iLevel)
    return;

  if (LoadString (sDebug.hInst, iFrmt, sDebug.sMsg, MAX_DEBUG_STR)
      <= 0)
    DebugPrint (iWin, "DebugPrintRes - No string: %d.. ", iFrmt);
  else
    {
    va_start (pVa, iFrmt);
    vDebugPrint (iWin, sDebug.sMsg, pVa);
    }
}

void vDebugPrintRes (int iWin,int iFrmt,void const *pVa)
{

  if (iLevel)
    return;

  if (LoadString (sDebug.hInst, iFrmt, sDebug.sMsg, MAX_DEBUG_STR)
      <= 0)
    DebugPrint (iWin, "vDebugPrintRes - No string: %d.. ", iFrmt);
  else
    vDebugPrint (iWin, sDebug.sMsg, pVa);
}

  #endif


  #endif
```

mda.c

```
#if DEBUG > 0
```

```
#define IBM_PRINTER

#define    NUM_ROWS            25
#define    NUM_COLS            80

// Defined here and in debgprn.c
#define      PRINT_SCREEN      0x01
#define      FILE_OFF          0x02
#define      PAUSE_OFF         0x04
#define      ERROR_OFF         0x08
#define      PAUSED            0x10


// you use these so you can use selectors in Windows.
// For DOS they never change.
unsigned uMonoBase=0xB000, uKeyBase=0x40;


FLAG MdaInit (void)
{
volatile BYTE _far *fpScrn;

#ifdef WIN
long lNum;

  // If you are in protected mode, you need to get selectors to the
  // video and BIOS RAM. These are magical values returned by
  // kernel.
  if (GetWinFlags () & WF_PMODE)
    {
    lNum = (long) GetProcAddress (GetModuleHandle
                        ((LPSTR) "KERNEL"), (LPSTR) "__B000h");
    if (LOWORD (lNum))
      uMonoBase = LOWORD (lNum);
    lNum = (long) GetProcAddress (GetModuleHandle
                        ((LPSTR) "KERNEL"), (LPSTR) "__0040h");
    if (LOWORD (lNum))
      uKeyBase = LOWORD (lNum);
    }
#endif

  // Test to see whether RAM at this location - if not - no MDA.
```

```c
    // If you pass, it simply means RAM, not necessarily an MDA.
    // However, because this is for debugging, ideally the
    // developer knows what he is doing.
    fpScrn = PTR (uMonoBase, 0);
    *fpScrn = 1;
    if (*fpScrn != 1)
      return (true);
    *fpScrn = 2;
    if (*fpScrn != 2)
      return (true);

    return (false);
}


// These calls are implemented in case you want to write a driver
// for another monitor that is not 80x25
int MdaNumRows (void)
{

  return (NUM_ROWS);
}

int MdaNumCols (void)
{

  return (NUM_COLS);
}

// This works even under Windows to beep
void MdaBeep (void)
{

  _asm
    {
    mov     ax, 0E07h
    mov     bx, 0007h
    int     10h
    }
}

// Fills the screen starting at row, col with the passed in
// character/attribute pair for num pairs.
```

```
void MdaFill (int iRow,int iCol,unsigned uChrAtr,int iNum)
{

   fMemwSet (PTR (uMonoBase, iRow*NUM_COLS*2+iCol*2), uChrAtr, iNum);
}


// Writes the passed-in string starting at row, col for num bytes.
void MdaWrite (int iRow,int iCol,BYTE const _far *pBuf,int iNum)
{
BYTE _far *fpScrn;

   fpScrn = PTR (uMonoBase, iRow * NUM_COLS * 2 + iCol * 2);
   while (iNum--)
     {
     *fpScrn = *pBuf++;
     fpScrn += 2;
     }
}


// Scrolls the screen up 1 line. The block at row+1, col -
// nr, nc is moved to row, col - nr-1, nc. The line at nr, nc
// is then filled with blanks.
void MdaScroll (int iRow,int iCol,int iNr,int iNc)
{
int iNum;
BYTE _far *fpScrn;

   fpScrn = PTR (uMonoBase, iRow * NUM_COLS * 2 + iCol * 2);
   for (iNum=0; iNum<iNr-1; iNum++)
     {
     fMemCpy (fpScrn, fpScrn+NUM_COLS*2, iNc * 2);
     fpScrn += NUM_COLS * 2;
     }

   // blank line
   MdaFill (iRow + iNr - 1, iCol, 0x0720, iNc);
}


// Returns the character/attribute pair at row, col. The character
// is in the low byte.
unsigned MdaGetChar (int iRow,int iCol)
{
```

```c
   return (*(unsigned _far *) PTR (uMonoBase, iRow * NUM_COLS * 2 +
         iCol * 2));
}

// Returns the toggle and shift key state. Windows only updates
// the Num Lock, alt, ctrl, and shift keys while you are printing
// to the MDA. Therefore, in windows, you use Num Lock instead of
// Scroll Lock to pause the MDA.

// Scroll Lock (Num Lock) - PAUSED
// Left Shift - PAUSE_OFF (Scroll Lock still works)
// Right Shift - PRINT_SCREEN
// Ctrl - FILE_OFF
// Alt - ERROR_OFF
BYTE MdaKey (void)
{
BYTE bTmp, bRtn;

  bTmp = *((BYTE far *) PTR (uKeyBase, 0x17));
  bRtn = 0;

#if WIN > 0
  if (bTmp & 0x20)
    bRtn = PAUSED;
#else
  if (bTmp & 0x10)
    bRtn = PAUSED;
#endif

  if (bTmp & 0x01)
    bRtn |= PRINT_SCREEN;
  if (bTmp & 0x02)
    bRtn |= PAUSE_OFF;
  if (bTmp & 0x04)
    bRtn |= FILE_OFF;
  if (bTmp & 0x08)
    bRtn |= ERROR_OFF;

  return (bRtn);
}
```

```
// Prints a character via int 17. This works under Windows
// although most networks won't send it on until you un-pause.
// you don't use DOS because it can't poll the printer status.
// Define IBM_PRINTER if your printer handles the full IBM
// character set. If not, you get | and - for the dividers but
// any other printed weird characters become spaces.
// Returns true on an error - and then printing stops.
FLAG MdaPrnt (BYTE bChr,FLAG fTran)
{

   // Do you need to translate the char?
   if (fTran)
     {
     // If your printer supports the full IBM character set - define
     // IBM_PRINTER and it will print all the characters.
#ifdef IBM_PRINTER
     if ((bChr == '\r') || (bChr == '\n'))
       bChr = ' ';
#else

     if ((bChr < 0x20) || (bChr >= 0x7F))
       switch (bChr)
           {
           case 0xB9 :
           case 0xBA :
           case 0xCC :
             bChr = '|';
             break;
           case 0xCA :
           case 0xCB :
           case 0xCD :
             bChr = '-';
             break;
           case 0xCE :
             bChr = '+';
             break;
           default :
             bChr = ' ';
             break;
           }
#endif
     }
```

```
    // Check status and then print if possible
    _asm
      {
      mov       ah, 01h
      xor       dx, dx
      int       17h
      mov       al, 1
      cmp       ah, 90h
      jne       err
      xor       ah, ah
      mov       al, bChr
      xor       dx, dx
      int       17h
      mov       al, 0
err:  mov    bChr, al
      }

    return (bChr);
}

#endif
```

INDEX

.EXE files, 93, 156
#else, 12
#endif, 11
#ifdefDEBUG, 11, 12, 73, 94
  and assertion code, 39
  and C++, 105
  and debugging in conditional defines, 21
  and MemCheck, 156
#ifs, 58-59
_AllocChkHeap, 73-75, 82
_AllocHeapWalk, 73-75
_AllocWalkHeap, 73
_end, 28
FILE, 29, 30, 87
  and assertion code, 42
  and open calls, 95
LINE, 29, 30, 87
  and assertion code, 42
  and open calls, 95
0x00, 33
0x7E, 33
0xFE, 33
0xFEFE, 43

Addresses
  and realloc, 16-17
  and stack space, 63
ah=68h, 31
ALLOC, 70, 71, 72, 85
  non-debug version of, 75-76
ALLOC_CHK2, 71
ALLOC_CHK1, 71
ALLOC_CHK3, 70
ALLOC_ID, 71
AllocCheck, 70, 80
AllocDone, 70, 81-82
AllocFree, 71, 77-79
AllocList, 70, 80, 81
AllocRealloc, 79-81
AllocSize, 71, 82
API (Application Program Interface)
  and the testing process, 137, 140
Arrays, 60
  and assertion code, 44, 46-47
ASCII, 45, 57, 93
ASM, 22, 32, 105

Assembly language, 25
  and IntTest, 113-15
  and local variables, creation of, 120-22
  and registers, checking of, 115-20, 122
  special tricks for, 113-23
  and Trap, 113-15
  and TrashReg, 119, 122
Assertion checking, 2, 82
  and assembly language, 122
  and AssertBool, 42-43
  and Assert code, 39-52
  and AssertEmsPtr, 90, 91-92
  and AssertHeapPtr, 82
  and asserting a structure, 45-48
  and AssertInt, 43-44
  and AssertPrintf, 42
  and AssertStr, 44-45
  base class, 110-12
  and conditional defines, 59
  and file I/O, 93, 94, 101
  and parameter validation, 49-51
  and Write, 101
Autoexec.bat, 129
Automation
  and Microsoft Test, 153-55
  and the testing process, 128-29, 133, 136, 137
AX, 115, 118

Base Assert, 110
Base Dump, 110-11
Basic, 154
Batch files, 153
Beta tests, 139-44, 145, 146, 147, 158
BIOS, 152
  and exiting, 28
  and stack space, 64
Bitmaps, 60
Black-box testing, 133, 134-35, 136
Boolean expressions
  and assertion code, 40, 42-43
Borland, 63, 161
Bounds Checker, 151-53, 163
  and CRC checking, 37
  and exiting, 28

BP, 120
Buffers, 21, 100, 103
  and assertion code, 39, 44-45
  filling of, 32-35
  and CRC checking, 37
  and freeing a structure, 33-34
  length of, 44-45
  and TrashReg, 119
Bug(s)
  count, total, 18
  definition of, 7-10
  -discovery tools, summary of, 151-66
  origins of, 8-9
  reports, 129, 143-44
  and severity levels, 130-31
BUGBUGs, 22, 23, 115
bugcheck.h, 61
BugLev, 60-61
Bug Master, 130, 131, 132
BugTyp, 60-61
Bulletin boards, 142, 145

C language, 4, 22, 25, 36, 105-7, 111
  and assembly language, 113, 115
  and assertion code, 41
  and Bounds Checker, 152
  and bug-discovery tools, 161
  and dynamic memory overwrites, 156
  and heap memory, 69
  and initialization, 28, 120
  local variables in, 120
  and NULL pointers, 35
  and OOP, 32
  and pointer bugs, 9
C++, 105-12
  and assembly language, 113
  and bug-discovery tools, 161
  and ENTER/EXIT logging, 30
  and OOP, 32
  underwriting and overwriting in, 106, 107-8, 109
Caching, 17
CASE, 7
Casting, 36

Character sets
  ASCII, 57
  English, 44
Check, 42
CheckBool, 42
Check Registers, 115-20, 122
CHECK_STACK, 116-17
Circuit boards, 36
Close, 102-4
COBOL, 9, 154
Code path(s), 14-16
  and assembly language, 113, 120
  and local variables, 120
  and low-level functions, 18
  and malloc, 14
  and the testing process, 133, 134, 135
  walking through each, 16
Code View, 57
Color video cards, 57
Comments, 21-23
Compilers, 18, 66
  and assertion code, 52
  and bug-discovery tools, 161-62
  and ENTER/EXIT logging, 30
  and stack space, 64
CompuServe, 142, 145
Conditional defines, 59-60
config.sys, 129
Consistency checks, 2-3
  and CRC checking, 37
  and file I/O, 93-94
CONST
  and CRC checking, 37
  prototyping including, 35-36
ConstReg, 119-20
Constructors, 107-12
Copying
  and EmsCopy, 90
Crash Analyzer, 158
CRC checking, 21, 37, 59
CTRL-C, 27
CX, 118

Database(s)
  and buffers, freeing of, 34
  and the testing process, 19, 130-32
DDE (dynamic data exchange)
  and the testing process, 138, 140, 154
debgmsg.c, 167-71
debgprnt.c, 181-91
DEBUG
  and assertion code, 40, 41, 45
  and conditional defines, 59
  proper use of, 13-14
  using the value of, 20
DEBUG_FILL_CHAR, 33
DebugMessageBox, 54, 55, 56, 58, 64, 112
DebugMessageRes, 54, 55
DebugPause, 58
DebugPrintfs, 11, 31, 55, 57-58, 61, 75, 112
Deletion, 34, 105, 106-7
Destructors, 107-12
DOS, 4, 17, 27, 83, 97
  and assertion code, 40-41
  and bug-discovery tools, 151, 152, 153, 154, 160,
    163, 164, 166
  and DebugMessageBox, 56
  and debug printfs, 54, 55, 57
  and error message files, 31
  and exiting, 28
  and file I/O, 97, 98, 100, 103
  and parameter validation, 51
  and Read, 100
  and stack space, 63
  and the testing process, 137, 138
  Version 3.3, 32
  Version 4.0, 31, 32
  Version 5.0, 148
DPMI (DOS Protected Mode Interface), 83
Dr. Watson, 158-59
Dump, 110-11
DX, 118

Edefine, 112
else, 14
EMS (expanded memory), 17
  and Bounds Checker, 152
  and exiting, 28
  and heap memory, 83, 84-92
EMSCheckHdl, 90-91
EmsCopy, 90
EnableFreeChecking, 159
EnableHeapChecking, 159
ENTER, 29-31
ENTER/EXIT logging, 29-31
Errno check, 97, 100, 101
Error message files, 31-32
ESC, 55
Exit, 28-31, 55
  and CTRL-C, 27
  ENTER/, logging, 29-31
  and NULL pointers, 35
  and testing the system, 27

File Already Exists error, 95
Filenames
  and heap memory, 70, 70, 83
  and the testing process, 134
File Doesn't Exist error, 95
Files Done, 104
FILL_CHAR, 89, 90, 92, 106
  and assembly language, 120
  and C++, 107, 109
Flags
  testing of, 20-21
free, 70, 71
fShowOK, 73
func1, 27
func2, 27
funcBad, 26-27
Functionality, 4
  and severity levels, 130
  and the testing process, 130, 134, 135, 141

Global variables, 25, 43, 46-47, 159
  and buffers, 35
  and C++, 105

  and exiting, 28
  and NULL pointers, 35
  and stack space, 63
Graphics, 4, 19, 165

Handle(s)
  -based calls, checking of, 97-98
  open file, and exiting, 28
  tracking of, 83-88
HANDLE_EMS, 89
HANDLE_NEXT, 84
Hdl, 95, 102
HdlAdd, 85-86
HdlCreate, 84-85
HdlDelete, 87-88
HdlExist, 86-87
HdlFind, 86-87, 97
HdlNext, 88
Heap memory, 28, 69-92
  and ALLOC, 71-81
  and the concepts behind the code, 69-70
  and EMS, 83, 84-92
  and handle tracking, 83-88
  and XMS, 84-88
Heap Walker, 159, 160

i++, 14
I/O (input/output), 17, 93-104
  and assertion checking, 93, 94, 101
  and buffers, freeing of, 34
  and consistency checking, 93-94
  and DOS, 97, 98, 100, 103
  and the Errno check, 97, 100, 101
  and handle-based calls, checking of, 97-98
  and memory, 94, 95, 97
IBM, 98
ICE, 161, 162, 163, 164
IDs, 34, 106, 108-9, 111
  and assertion code, 45-47
  and buffers, 32-33
  and conditional defines, 59
if, 14, 15
IfDebug, 61
ifdef, 21

iFileLine, 71
iLine, 75
Informational messages, 53
Initialization
  of buffers, 32
  and C++, 108, 109
  and EMS, 89
  and exiting, 28
  of local variables, 63, 66-68, 120
  of strings, 45
inst.Assert(), 110
int, 14, 15
  and assertion code, 41, 42, 43-44
  and debug printfs, 57
  and prototyping including CONST, 35
Integers, 18
Intel, 161
Interrupt tables
  and exiting, 28
IntTests, 14-15, 21, 112, 133
  and assembly language, 113-15
  and walking through each code path, 16

jc (jmp if carry), 114-15

Keyboard input
  and Microsoft Test, 154

Libraries
  and CRC checking, 37
  and ENTER/EXIT logging, 31
  and MemCheck, 156
Linked list management, 18
Linker
  and code swapping, 17
Link errors
  and heap memory, 73
Literals, 44
Local variables
  creation of, 120-22
  initialization of, 63, 66-68, 120

Logic errors, 19, 22
  and assertion code, 52
  and exiting, 28
Loose pointers
  and CRC checking, 37
Lotus, 138
LPT1, 57

Macros
  and assembly language, 114-15, 116
  and assertion code, 40, 42
  definition of, inside a #ifdefDEBUG, 12
  and ENTER/EXIT logging, 29-31
  and exercising code paths, 14
Malloc, 14, 84, 105
  and assertion code, 44-45
  and C++, 106
  and debugging in conditional defines, 21
  and heap memory, 75, 83
  and prototyping including CONST, 36
  and stack space, 64
  testing of, for returning a NULL, 17. *See also*
    Memory, malloc'ed
Mapping
  and Bounds Checker, 151-52
  and heap memory, 89, 90-91
mc_register, 156
MDA (Monochrome Display Adapter), 57-58,
  59, 166
mda.c, 57, 191-97
MED records, 158
MemCheck, 151, 155-57
memCpy, 34, 36, 50-51, 156
Memory, 9, 17, 25, 34, 70, 75, 83
  and assertion functions, 94
  and buffers, filling of, 33
  and BUGBUGs, 22
  and bug-discovery tools, 159, 160, 162, 164
  and C++, 106
  and conditional defines, 21
  and DOS, 27
  and error message files, 31
  expanded (EMS), 17, 28, 83, 84-92, 152

extended (XMS) 28, 83, 84-88, 92
  and file I/O, 94, 95, 97
  and garbage data, 16-17
  overwrites, dynamic, 156
  and parameter validation, 50
  and stack space, 63, 64, 66
  and the testing process, 137, 139
  malloc'ed, 50, 69-71, 77, 80, 81, 84-85, 87, 89,
    152, 155-56
  mapping, 151-52
  video, 57, 152. *See also* Heap memory
Message Boxes, 55, 167-80
  and assertion code, 42
  and C++, 106
  debgmsg.c, 167-71
  and debug printfs, 53, 54-55
  and file I/O, 95, 97, 101
  and heap memory, 85, 89
  and MemCheck, 156
  pop_box.c, 172-76
  tty_box.c, 176-80
Message Bugs, 100
Microsoft, 161, 162
Microsoft C7, 63, 64, 66, 141
Microsoft Test, 151, 153-55
Monitors
  and debug printfs, 54
  and Microsoft Test, 154
  monochrome, 54, 57, 181-97
Motherboards, 129
Mouse input
  and Microsoft Test, 154
Multiscope, 157-58, 161, 165, 166

Naming conventions
  and open calls, 94
new, 105, 106-7
NODISCARD, 70, 78
NOMOVE, 78
Non-debug mode
  and C++, 105
  and heap memory, 70, 73, 75, 85, 89
Norton, 151

Nu-Mega, 151, 152
NULL, 13, 35
  and C++, 110
  and conditional defines, 59
  and heap memory, 70, 78, 86
  and MemCheck, 156
  memory locations, and TestAll, 25
  and open calls, 94
  and parameter validation, 50
  returning a, testing mallocs for, 17
NUM LOCK, 57

OLE (Object linking and embedding)
  and the testing process, 138, 140, 154
On/off propositions, 21
OOP (object oriented programming), 32
Open calls, 94-96
Open issues, 21-23
OS/2, 140, 165

Parameter(s), 13
  and assembly language, 116
  and buffers, 32
  and conditional defines, 59
  and debug printfs, 54, 57
  and file I/O, 97
  incorrect, and debug checking, 11
  and using variables, 60
  validation, 49-51
  and walking through each code path, 16
Periscope, 161, 162-63, 166
pFile, 75
pFileName, 71
pNextAlloc, 71
pop_box.c, 172-76
Post-Mortem Debugger, 157-58
pPrevAlloc, 71
printfs, 53-61
  and assertion code, 42
  conditional, 54, 59-61
  and ENTER/EXIT logging, 29, 31
  and exercising code paths, 14
  and MemCheck, 156

and Message box functions, 53, 54-55
and using variables, 60-61
Printing, 20, 57
and assertion code, 42
and BUGBUGs, 22, 115. *See also* printfs
Priority lists, 10
Prodigy, 98
Protection, 159
Prototyping, 7, 35-36

RAM, 17, 31, 93
and the testing process, 137, 139
Read, 36, 98, 99-101, 163
Reagan, Ronald, 100
realloc, 16-17, 70, 78, 79-81
Redefinition code, 105
RegCheck, 116, 122
RegEntry, 116
Registers, checking of, 115-20, 122
Reports, 129, 143-44
ROM BIOS, 55, 129
RT-Link, 17, 160-61

Scoping
and ENTER/EXIT logging, 30
Screen mode switching, 55
SCROLL LOCK, 57
SDK (Software Development Kit), 159, 161
Seek, 98-100
Semaphores, 17
Separability, 32
Severity levels, 130-31
Sharing bits sets, 94
Sharing violations, 97
Shipping, 142, 145-49
Soft-Ice, 15, 161, 162, 163-64, 166
Source code, 6, 40, 133
Spelling, 147
Stack space, 29, 63-68
and assertion code, 43
and Bounds Checker, 152
and exiting, 28
STACK_OFF, 116

StackUsed, 28
Startup code
and CRC checking, 37
and stack space, 66
stckfill.c, 65
stckused.c, 65
strcpy, 18, 19, 30, 36, 50, 156
Stress Applicator, 159, 160
String(s)
and assertion code, 40, 41-42, 44-45
and bug-discovery tools, 159
and C++, 108-9
constructors, 108
and debug printfs, 54
destructors, 109
initialization of, 45
and MemCheck, 156
and String Assert, 111-12
strlen, 19, 156
Structs
ALLOC, 71, 72
and assertion code, 41, 42
and local variables, 120
Sys_Critical_Init, 163
System state
restoration of, 27

TASKMODAL, 55
TestAll, 25-27
and CRC checking, 37
and exiting, 28
and heap memory, 89
and MemCheck, 156
and NULL pointers, 35
use of, illustration of, 27
Testing process, 125-44
and alpha testers, 141
and automation, 128-29, 133, 136, 137
and the beta test, 135, 139-44, 145, 146, 147
and black-box testing, 133, 134-35, 136
and the bug database, 130-32, 135
and bug reports, 129, 143-44
and designing tests, 135-36
and internal testing, 133, 141-42

and management, 147-48
and manual tests, 128, 133, 136
and regression testing, 129, 145, 146
and running tests, 136-37
setting up of, 126-27
and shipping, 142, 145-49
success of, elements of, 133
and testing plans, 127-38
and testing platforms, 137-38
and white-box testing, 133-34, 136
TestNull, 35
Text searches, 22
Trap, 14-15, 16, 21, 113-15
TRAPc, 114
TrapNot, 15
Traps, 111, 133
TrashReg, 119, 122
TSR (Terminate and Stay Resident), 5, 17
  and Bounds Checker, 152
  and stack space, 63, 64
  and the testing process, 137, 139, 140
tty_box.c, 176-80
Type-checking, 120

uChk, 71
uID, 45-47
UMB (Upper Memory Block), 137
Unerase, 151
Unrecoverable Application Error, 27
User interface
  and the testing process, 135
uSize, 71, 84

ValidateCodeSegments, 25, 159
ValidateFreeSpaces, 25, 159
VERBOSE, 59
Virtual functions, 106

VisiCalc, 151
Visual Basic, 154
VM_MURPHY, 160
void*, 36

Warning message, 36, 50
White-box testing, 133-34, 136
Win-Ice, 161, 164
Windows, 4, 151, 153-55
  and assertion code, 42
  and CRC checking, 37
  and debug printfs, 57
  debug version, 159-60
  and Dr. Watson, 158-59
  Enhanced Mode, 37
  MessageBox, 55
  and Multiscope, 165
  NUM LOCK, 57
  and parameter validation, 49
  Periscope for, 163
  Soft-Ice for (Win-Ice), 161, 164
  Software Development Kit (SDK), 159, 161
  and stack space, 63
  Standard Mode, 37
  and the testing process, 137-38, 140
  using DebugMessageBox in, 56
  Version 3.0, 50
  Version 3.1, 50, 148, 158, 159
WndProcs, 57
Word processing, 10, 19, 138
Word-size registers, 120
WordStar, 93
Write, 98, 101-2

XMS (extended memory)
  and exiting, 28
  and heap memory, 83, 84-88, 92

NO BUGS!
SOURCE DISK

To receive a disk containing the source code for *NO BUGS!* and the sample programs described in the book, please fill in the coupon below (or a copy thereof) and mail it with a check or money order, payable to *WTB Software*, to:

WTB Software
Suite 325
15127 N.E. 24th
Redmond, Washington 98052

The disk contains the following items:

- Full Source code to all examples in the book
- Complete library of No Bugging functions
- Source to basic c run-time library with full parameter checking

— —

Please send me the companion disk for *NO BUGS!*

Name: _____

Address: _____

City: _____ State: _____ Zip: _____

☐ 3.5 inch (default)
☐ 5.25 inch

Send me_____copies at $39 each: _____
Shipping outside USA, add $4.95/disk: _____
TOTAL: _____